OZARK HIGHLANDS
TRAIL GUIDE
#7

TIM ERNST

TIM ERNST PHOTOGRAPHY & PUBLISHING
JASPER, ARKANSAS
WWW.TIMERNST.COM

*The cover photo is of an eastern screech owl, commonly heard in evenings
along the OHT—one of the smallest owls in the USA and can fit in the palm of
your hand! Listen carefully to hear their beautiful soft music.
Photo by Tim Ernst*

Printed in the USA since 1988!
ISBN: 978-1882906-192

Some additional books by Tim Ernst

Arkansas Waterfalls guidebook
Arkansas Nature Lover's guidebook
Arkansas Hiking Trails guidebook
Buffalo River Hiking Trails guidebook
Ouachita Trail guidebook
Arkansas Dayhikes For Kids guidebook
Arkansas Greatest Hits picture book
Arkansas Splendor picture book
Arkansas Beauty picture book
Arkansas In My Own Backyard picture book
A Rare Quality Of Light picture book
Arkansas Nightscapes picture book
Buffalo River Beauty picture book
Arkansas Landscapes II picture book
Arkansas Portfolio III picture book
Arkansas Wildlife picture book
Arkansas Autumn picture book
Arkansas Waterfalls picture book
Arkansas Landscapes picture book
Buffalo River Dreams picture book
Arkansas Portfolio II picture book
Arkansas Wilderness picture book
Arkansas Spring picture book
Buffalo River Wilderness picture book
Wilderness Reflections picture book
Arkansas Portfolio picture book
The Search For Haley
The Cloudland Journal

Books can be found in retail stores throughout the region
and usual online outlets—best is www.UAPress.com.

TIM ERNST PHOTOGRAPHY & PUBLISHING
www.TimErnst.com

This guidebook is dedicated to **Roy Senyard** (1945-2018), longtime maintenance coordinator of the OHT who toiled for 30 years to keep the trail open and enjoyable for all hikers. Keep Roy's vision alive by kicking fallen limbs and stones off the trail, picking up trash, and leaving your campsite look like no one had ever been there. R. I. P. my friend...

Roy Senyard Falls, near mile 36 below the Ozark Highlands Trail

FOREWORD

Arkansas is blessed with extraordinary natural resources: beautiful mountains and forests, clean water, and abundant wildlife. But one of the most splendid assets in our state is the one million acre Ozark National Forest, created by President Theodore Roosevelt in 1908.

It is no exaggeration to say that the Ozark Highlands Trail, which runs 164 miles through the heart of the Forest, is one of the great scenic hiking trails in America. The vistas from White Rock Mountain, the waterfalls, and the many creeks and campgrounds make hiking the Ozarks one of the greatest experiences going.

In addition to appreciating the scenery, you will also notice that the trails you'll travel are unusually well maintained. We in Arkansas take great pride in our natural resources, and are committed to maintaining them as God surely intended. You can help the Ozark Highlands Trail Association and the National Forest Service preserve the Ozarks' beauty by following posted regulations and your own common sense.

So I hope that you enjoy this guide, and have a great hike. It's the best introduction that I know of to Arkansas, "The Natural State."

Dale Bumpers
former Governor, United States Senator,
and all around good egg...

Dale Bumpers was always a great friend of trails, outdoor recreation and the environment. While Governor he had a hand in the formation of the Arkansas Trails Council. As a United States Senator he was one of the main supporters of the Arkansas Wilderness Bill in 1984. Even in retirement he continued to work on the issues that affect our planet until his death in 2016. He was a great man, a wise old owl, and we were lucky to have had him on our side.

TABLE OF CONTENTS

OHT TRAIL DESCRIPTIONS AND MAPS by section

INTRODUCTION

ABOUT THIS GUIDE

The Ozark Highlands Trail (OHT) is truly one of the most outstanding hiking trails in the United States. *Backpacker* magazine has rated it as one of the Top 10 most scenic hiking trails in the USA! This guide contains all of the information that you will need in order to have a safe, informative and enjoyable hike on it. This is the latest edition of the guide (2021), and contains the most up-to-date information, plus it has separate sections with maps and descriptions of other trails that connect to the OHT. You will also find GPS coordinates for trailheads, roads, and streams (see page 154-156).

The first thing you should do is to sit down and read the whole thing, cover to cover. A lot of the information in this introduction will help you through the descriptive sections. For example, you will see "SSS" written in many places. Unless you read the glossary of terms you'll never know what that means, and you will miss a lot! Once you are familiar with this guide, you will be able to pull whatever information you need out of it in quick order.

The description of the OHT is divided into 12 sections (sections 1-11, plus the Sylamore Section of the OHT). At the beginning of each section is a map, elevation profile and mileage log (covering *both* directions), then a running description of the trail from *west to east*. I have hiked the entire trail many times and find this direction the most comfortable to hike.

Another reason why the description runs this way is because I actually sat down one day with a pile of topo maps and figured out the elevation gains, from end to end, going both directions. When you hike from west to east you have to climb about 200 feet *less* — and this is important. It's also nice to begin your hike each day heading into the sun. If you hike it the other way, there is a mileage log at the front of each section that shows the mileage from *east* to *west*, as well as a log for the entire trail going both directions on pages 32–34.

The OHT is part of the "Trans-Ozarks Trail" system that will one day extend from Lake Ft. Smith State Park all the way to St. Louis, Missouri — nearly 700 miles of trail! Where the original/classic OHT route ends at Woolum (mile 164), you can now continue downstream along the OHT/Buffalo River Trail

Extension for 43.6 miles to Dillards Ferry Trailhead/Hwy 14—a continuous 207.6 miles of great hiking trail!

One day the trail will continue downstream from Hwy. 14 through the Lower Buffalo Wilderness and connect with the Sylamore section of the Ozark National Forest (see the map and description of the 31.6 mile Sylamore section on page 140). Other trail sections are being built the full length of Lake Norfork that will go to the Arkansas/Missouri border* and connect with the Ozark Trail in Missouri, eventually ending up in St. Louis. You may need a longer vacation to do all of that in one hike!

*Total amount of trail in Arkansas will be about 317 miles, give or take. I plan to detail each of the new sections/gaps in upcoming versions of this guide until we reach Missouri.

Please forgive me if some of the language in this guide sounds a little odd — I have lived in the Ozarks all of my life, and, well, I sometimes write the same way that I talk! 'Nuff said.

HISTORY

The OHT was dedicated as a National Recreation Trail in 1984. The original length was 165 miles (ending at Woolum, what I call the **"original/classic route"**), shortened to 164 miles, then 43.6 miles were added in 2021 via the Buffalo River Trail Extension for a total continuous trail of 207.6 miles. The Sylamore Section of the OHT added 31.6 miles, but it currently is not connected to the main trail yet (there are gaps on either end).

But we didn't get to this point overnight. Construction of the OHT was begun in 1977 with funding from the U.S. Forest Service. It continued 'til 1981 when, with only a third of the trail complete, the funding ran out. Up to this time the trail was built by various youth groups, including YACC and YCC groups. The trail was not blazed or signed. In fact, many sections were not even connected to any access points — like even a forest road. There was little use on the trail. Few hikers even knew it existed.

I had been involved with the Forest Service for many years, knew about the trail construction, and was always eager to hike each new section as it was completed. I became aware of the loss of funding through Arkansas Trails Council meetings. These quarterly meetings bring land managers like the Forest Service and users like me together to discuss trail opportunities, and problems. It was obvious that this wonderful trail that had been started was in danger of fading into the forest if something was not done. And it was also obvious that there was no money available to help the trail, so any work that was to be done would have to come from volunteers.

OZARK HIGHLANDS TRAIL ASSOCIATION

In the fall of 1981 I called a meeting of the folks in the area who were interested in hiking. I felt that if we could come up with a dozen people who would help me do some work on the trail that maybe we could save it, why even extend it, and goodness sakes, someday even complete it.

I was shocked when more than fifty people showed up at that first meeting. Before the night had ended, the Ozark Highlands Trail Association (OHTA) was formed, and we were on our way. In less than a year we were working on the trail every month, were publishing a monthly newsletter, and had several hundred members, all of us being volunteers.

Since then thousands of OHTA volunteers have contributed hundreds of thousands of hours of labor to the trail. OHTA has members in many states; have work trips, hikes and meetings all year; has received many awards, including several national awards; and is an affiliate club of the American Hiking Society, the only national voice for hikers.

OHTA was organized to *"Build, Maintain and Enjoy the OHT."* We try to be involved with every phase of the trail, from the initial planning stages through to the completed product. We work closely with the Forest Service on all of this, and have had a good relationship with them over the years. We have come a long way since the days when they used to "hide" the trail and clearcut large sections of it. And we still have a long way to go.

OHTA will continue to be the driving force behind this trail for many years to come. The club depends on donations and other support from hikers, especially volunteer maintainers!

Ozark Highlands Trail Association
P. O. Box 4065
Fayetteville, AR 72702
ohta@OzarkHighlandsTrail.com
Web page—**www.OzarkHighlandsTrail.com**
OHTA is a nonprofit 501c-3 organization, and donations are tax–deductible! Get involved—volunteer.

If you hike this trail, you should join and support OHTA.

FOREST SERVICE, Ozark National Forest

Most of the original OHT is on Ozark National Forest property (sections 1–8). It crosses three ranger districts. Each of these districts is responsible for their own section, and in many cases they manage it quite differently. The offices are closed on weekends, so arrive at the trailhead prepared with all the info you need.

There is a protected corridor two hundred feet on either side the entire length of the trail where timber management practices are generally prohibited. Sometimes sections of the trail may be closed due to a controlled burn in the area, especially during January—April, but this can happen at any time and without notice. If you are planning a long-distance hike you might want to contact the districts you will be hiking across ahead of time to see if they have any burns scheduled that may close the trail. And/or plan to hike around the burn area if needed.

Forest service offices (www.fs.usda.gov/osfnf):

Boston Mtn. District	Big Piney Ranger District
P.O. Box 76 (Hwy. 23 N.)	12000 SR 27
Ozark, AR 72949	Hector, AR 72843
479–667–2191	479–284–3150
Pleasant Hill District	Big Piney Ranger District
P.O. Box 190 (Hwy. 21 N.)	P.O. Box 427 (Hwy. 7 N.)
Clarksville, AR 72830	Jasper, AR 72641
479–754–2864	870–446–5122

NATIONAL PARK SERVICE, Buffalo National River

The OHT Buffalo River Trail Extension from Woolum to Dillards Ferry (43.6 miles, sections 9-11, competed in 2021), is part of the Buffalo National River and is managed by the National Park Service in Harrison. Many folks think of the Buffalo for floating, but it has a terrific system of hiking trails!

The main visitor contact locations are the Tyler Bend Visitor Center at Silver Hill (Middle District) and Buffalo Point Recreation Area (Lowe District) downstream of Hwy. 14. They *are* open on weekends and provide full visitor info services.

Find tons of great info here: www.nps.gov/buff

Tyler Bend Visor Center 870–439–2502

Buffalo Point Info Station 870–449–4311

ARKANSAS STATE PARKS, Lake Ft. Smith State Park

The OHT begins at Lake Ft. Smith State Park, and the first five miles of the trail are managed by them. They have always been supportive of the trail and are proud that it begins there.

The original state park (and the beginning of the OHT) was closed in 2002 to make way for a new lake to service the city of Ft. Smith. The new park opened in 2007, and along with it a new beginning trailhead for the OHT.

Lake Ft. Smith State Park, 479–369–2469
www.ArkansasStateParks.com

Arkansas State Parks also serve the hiking community through the Arkansas Trails Council.
www.ArkansasTrailsCouncil.com

CAMPING

Once you get out of the state park at mile 5.3 on the OHT you are on either national forest or national park service land and camping is allowed anywhere at least a half mile outside of the recreation areas. You should camp at least 200 feet away from the trail and any water sources though—except you *are* allowed to camp on gravel bars along the Buffalo National River, yea!

There are eight campgrounds along or near the original OHT. These are: Lake Ft. Smith, White Rock Mountain, Shores Lake, Redding, Ozone, Haw Creek Falls, Fairview and Richland Creek. All of them have tables, water (usually not in winter), and toilets. Lake Ft. Smith, Shores Lake and Redding have showers in the summer. Several charge a fee, and have other facilities. Some are closed during the winter months. Campgrounds along the OHT/ BRT extension are at Tyler Bend, S. Maumee, and Spring Creek.

LOW IMPACT USE

As the OHT gets more and more use, we need to be especially careful that we don't impact the special areas along it. It's easy to destroy a fragile spot, but it's just as easy to tread lightly and keep from messing up the things that we came out to see in the first place. All it takes is a little common sense. If we all do our part, this wonderful trail of ours will stay that way so that generations to follow will be able to enjoy the raw scenic beauty as we have. Here are a few guidelines to follow:

Stay on the trail. The OHT was designed to carry you from one point to another in the most efficient (and/or scenic) way. When folks cut switchbacks, erosion begins, and soon the trail is messed up and there is an ugly scar. It is not rude to ask someone that you see doing this to kindly get back on the trail.

Hike in small groups. It's fun to go out with a large gang, but that doesn't always work well in the backcountry — it destroys the character and solitude of the place, not to mention increasing the possibility of damage to the trail and surrounding areas. Always limit the size of your group to 10 or less when you're going to be camping. Fewer is generally better. Besides, you'll have more campsite selection if you only have one or two tents to set up! Have your parties at home — come to the woods to enjoy nature, not Billboard's Top Ten. Speaking of noise, be considerate of others — they just might be out on the trail to get away from all the hustle and bustle of city life — enjoy the peaceful solitude, and let others do the same.

Camp in established sites when possible. Overnight stays have more impact on the land than probably anything else we do while hiking. If everyone camped in a new location every night, the damage would be much more widespread. By concentrating this damage to several sites, the area will stay more primitive. If you must set up in a new spot, choose a site at least 200 feet *away from the trail* and any water source, and preferably out of sight (*and please, please don't build a new fire ring*). I hate to hike down a nice trail and see tents scattered along the way. Don't you?

Protect our water. Clean water adds so much to the outdoor experience, not to mention our quality of life in general. Here is a simple guideline to remember when in the backcountry — don't put *anything* into the water. Period! I know, I know, you use "biodegradable soap." What if the guy just upstream is using it too, and takes a bath in the creek that you're getting your kool aid water out of? You'll have suds in your punch! Oh yea, it will be biodegradable punch, but suds just the same. Yuk! Think about downstream — we all live there. Use biodegradable soap if you have to, but use it *away* from the stream. Or better yet, don't use soap of any kind.

Keep bathroom duties out of sight. This seems rather obvious, but not everyone seems to understand. You need to get completely out of sight of the trail and any water supply to do your business. Dig a small hole, fill it in and cover it up when you're done. Why do people still leave their mess next to the trail?

Cook with a stove. We haven't reached a firewood shortage yet along the OHT, but if we all built big fires every day we would have one. Do all of your cooking with one of the lightweight stoves available — they're quicker and a whole lot cleaner anyway. Campfires are OK, but keep them *small*, don't build a fire ring, and only use dead branches that are on the ground and that you can break with you hands — if you have to saw it, it's too darn big! (Large wood seldom ever burns up completely, and what you have left over is an ugly black stick.)

Leave No Trace. This should be your goal on any trip on a trail, no matter where it is — when you leave there should be no sign of your ever having been there. It really seems silly to even mention this, but because there are still a few stupid people in the woods, I will. *Pack It In, Pack It Out* — don't litter! Don't carve up trees. Don't cut or destroy *any* living thing. Leave it as you found it. In fact, leave it cleaner than you found it — carry a trash bag for not only your own stuff, but for other litter that you see along the way.

FIRES

Open fires are allowed on the OHT, and permits are not required. *But new fire rings are **not** allowed*! If you aren't camping in an area that already has a fire ring, then please don't build one. It isn't really necessary, and the blackened rocks will be an ugly scar for a long time.

There is usually plenty of dead wood already on the ground for a normal fire. Don't cut trees of any kind. And if you are in a popular area, you may have to roam out a little further to find enough wood, but there is plenty. Of course, it is best to simply carry a backpacker's stove and not worry about it. Keeps your pots a lot cleaner too!

To build a low–impact fire, first clear away all of the leaves and other duff, down to bare dirt. Build a small fire in the middle of the cleared–out area. Use dead branches that are on the ground, not broken from tree trunks. I usually build a "pile fire" — add alternate layers of leaves and small twigs. As the leaves burn, the twigs will too. Gradually add bigger twigs 'til they will

14

burn each other. It's not too pretty, and does get a little smoky, but it's the fastest and easiest way to build a small fire.

When you are finished, and this is the most important step of all, make sure that your fire is *completely out*. Drown it, stir it, drown it, and stir it again. You've all seen those Smoky the Bear commercials. He isn't kidding. It's a shame to burn down a wonderful forest. And guess what, if you accidently start a forest fire, *you* may get a bill for what it cost to put it out! You should be able to lay your hand on the fire and not feel **any** heat. Once you're convinced that it's dead out, cover the area with leaves and twigs so that you can't tell you've built a fire there.

WATER

Most of the time you will cross water many, many times during the day on the OHT. There are only a few bridges on the trail—you can usually cross the smaller creeks without getting wet, larger creeks will require "wet" crossings but are doable. There are a exceptions of course, and these are noted in the descriptions. March through June is the wet season here, and you may have to wade more often then. Just be careful and take it easy. I have found that the best, and lightest footwear to wear when wading is a wool sock. Not only does it save your feet from rock cuts, but you get to wash your socks at the same time!

A note of caution here. Prolonged heavy rains often cause many of the streams to flood, and it can be *extremely* dangerous crossing during this time. This can happen any time of the year. As I am writing this, the story of a hiker who drowned while on the OHT is on the front page of the newspaper (see page 78). Anyway, when you do cross swollen streams, be sure to unbuckle the hip belt on your backpack — this will make it easier to get out of the pack if you should happen to get swept away. *Rushing water two feet deep can knock a hiker down!*

The water is generally clean and free of pollution. But that doesn't mean that it won't make you sick. There are lots of tiny critters that are swimming around in the water that may not match what your system is used to. If I were you, I would be sure and treat all the water that I drink out on the trail.

There are some sections of the trail that don't have much water. These are also noted in the descriptions. And of course we do have a dry period here. Usually in August and September most of the small streams dry up. The creeks on the map that have names do have water most of the time, though you may have to hunt up or downstream to find it. I have seen a time when there was virtually no water on the entire trail. This is rare, but it does happen. Check with me before your trip, or the District Ranger's office for that section.

HIKING PACE

The question that I get asked most is "how far can I hike in a day?" That is a good question, and no one knows the answer to that except *you*. How far or how fast you hike is determined by so many different factors, the least of which is the trail (most people think that they can hike a lot faster with a full backpack than they really can). The OHT is built to standards which enable most folks to hike it with no problem. You may have to slow down a little going up a hill, but there are only a few really steep sections, and again these are noted in the descriptions.

Generally speaking, if you are an average hiker, including rest stops and lunch, you can probably average about a mile an hour when you are carrying a backpack. Most folks who don't *backpack* much, and there is a big difference between backpacking and just hiking with no weight on your back, can hike six to ten miles a day without too much trouble. Although it has been my experience that for most people, less miles and more time to look around is best. The typical hiker, in great shape, can do the OHT end–to–end in about two weeks. It takes longer for some, shorter for others. It all depends on you! *Don't overestimate your ability.*

If you are in good shape, hike a lot, and aren't interested in spending a great deal of time messing around, sure you can hike fifteen or more miles a day. When I go out and get serious, I average about three miles an hour, and typically cover twenty plus miles a day. But, of course, it hurts.

When it is cold out you tend to start hiking with too many clothes on, and soon break out in a sweat. *This can kill you*, and you may not even realize what is happening! Of course I'm talking about hypothermia. I'm not going to tell you all about it, or how to treat it — you should read up on it though before you go into the woods. I will say this — use the layering method when you hike, i.e. remove clothing as you get warm, and always hike so that you don't work up a sweat (slow down your pace if you have to). In fact, I always start off feeling slightly chilled knowing that my motor (and the hill ahead!) will heat things up soon enough.

WILDLIFE, INCLUDING BEARS AND SNAKES

There is an abundance of wildlife along the trail, both large and small. I have seen everything from colorful lizards and hummingbirds to bald eagles, bears and elk. Most of these critters, though, will flee at the first sign (or noise) of a hiker, so you probably won't see a whole lot while you are hiking. But when you stop and take time out, that is another story.

I'm not much of a bird person, but I can tell you that there are dozens and dozens of different species out there. My favorite ones are the eagles of course. Which, by the way, you are likely to see during the winter on any part of the trail, though the Lake Ft. Smith and Lake Shepherd Springs areas are the best bets. There are now grouse being stocked in several areas near the trail. I haven't seen any yet, but am looking forward to it!

Yes, there are **bears**. Black bears were reintroduced in the 1960's by the Game and Fish Commission. They are not the huge grizzly bears that you hear and see so much of on TV though. They are pretty small, actually about the same size as you and me. They aren't really much of a problem — yet. We have only had one incident of physical harm to a hiker that I'm aware of (see page 61). The bear population continues to increase (and there is a bear season each fall), but still bear sightings are rare.

Most bears will take off just as fast as they can, if they see or scent you. Any loud noise will usually send a curious one off into the woods in a hurry. If you see a bear, and it is obvious that he has seen you, shout at the top of your lungs. That sounds easy, but I wonder how much breath you would have left if the critter is right on top of you? Bang on pots if you can't scream. If that doesn't work, good luck.

Even though bears have not been much of a problem in the past, that doesn't mean that you can ignore them. They are strong, and under the wrong circumstances, can be quite dangerous. Although it's probably not a necessity to "bear bag" your food when you camp, it's a good idea. *Do not keep food in the tent with you* though. I use a bear–proof container now to keep my food in, and to stash at mid–way trailheads. They work

17

great, and are no trouble, except for the extra weight.

And yes, there are snakes. Lots of snakes. Copperheads. Rattlesnakes. And cottonmouths. And they do bite (I've been bitten by a copperhead myself, but it was a dry bite). But no deaths have been reported that I know of. Bees kill more people nationwide than snakes do. But they are there. Watch out for them. Look at them. But for goodness sakes don't play with them. A snake will not seek you out and bite you. If you reach down and pick one up, or happen to step on one, sure it will bite you. What else can it do? Watch your step and mind your own business and you shouldn't have any problems.

If you do happen to get bit, the best thing that you can do is relax, you probably aren't going to die. And get to a doctor as soon as you can. Most people don't know how to use a snakebite kit so they aren't much good, but I do recommend that you carry a device called "The Extractor" — it does work (on bee stings too). The main thing is to just try and stay out of their way.

HUNTING AND FISHING

The Ozark National Forest is one of the best places to hunt in this part of the country. And the OHT goes right down the middle of it! Many people are afraid to be on the trail during hunting seasons (understandable), but those also some of the best times to be on the trail hiking. NOTE that the Buffalo National River is also open to hunting.

There are few conflicts between hunters and hikers — we all seem to share the trail well. And it was built for everyone to use (foot traffic that is). If you are concerned about hunters, find out when the seasons are, wear blaze orange and make a lot of noise. Although I wouldn't carry a "ghetto blaster" with me while on the trail, 'cause that might draw fire. I try to avoid hiking early or late in the day, which is when hunters are most active.

The most popular species are squirrel, deer, turkey and bear. The Arkansas Game and Fish Commission has a great management program, and the populations of game are at an all time high. They work in cooperation with the Forest Service in the forest near the trail to keep these populations strong. You will see several wildlife food plots and ponds along the trail. These are built especially to help out with both the game and non–game animals during the winter.

Fishing is good in some areas, but unfortunately the streams are generally not large enough to support a whole lot of fish. Lake Ft. Smith, Shores Lake, the Mulberry River and the Big Piney River all have good fishing. And a lot of the other streams will give you lots of thrills when using ultralight tackle. But I wouldn't count on eating fish during a hike.

Hunting and fishing licenses are required of all resident and nonresident sportsmen. For current information contact:

The Arkansas Game and Fish Commission
2 Natural Resources Drive
Little Rock, AR 72205
501–223–6300, www.agfc.com

REGULATIONS

There aren't many regulations that pertain just to the OHT, but the Forest Service does have a lot of them for the Forest in general. There is always a copy of these posted in the campgrounds and at other trailheads. You do not need a permit to hike on the trail (or build a fire), and dogs are allowed on the first 164 miles, but they must be on a leash when in a recreation area **(NOTE: dogs are not allowed on the trail past mile 164)**.

Horses, pack stock, motorized vehicles, and mountain bikes are not currently allowed on the trail (however there is mounting pressure to allow mountain bikes). The OHT is just not built or maintained for this type of travel. There are other trails in the state that will accommodate them. We do have some limited horse and four–wheeler use, and associated damage on the trail. One of the biggest problems is that they cause a lot of confusion — especially when a four–wheeler trail intersects with the OHT. When the trail follows an old road bed watch for intersections.

I get a lot of questions about guns. Yes, they are allowed. No, they are not necessary. If you feel that you want to carry one for "protection," then check with the Game and Fish Commission for their regulations. Most of the trail is within either the White Rock or the Big Piney Wildlife Management Areas, and guns may not be allowed except during the hunting seasons.

And that is about it. The other "do's and don'ts" are just common sense things. Don't build fire rings. Or camp near water or the trail. Or dump *anything* into the water. Bury your waste. Be a clean camper. Be considerate of your fellow hikers who are also out there for a little solitude. *Pack It In — Pack It Out*. I'm sorry, this *is* a must. Litter is just not done on the OHT. Don't leave anything behind, and do pick up what you see that shouldn't be there. We always carry a trash bag on our hikes, and try to leave the trail a little cleaner than how we found it. I hope that you do too.

TRAIL REGISTERS

There are trail registers on every district and scattered all along the original/classic trail. It is important that you sign in every time that you pass one of these. Yes, it is helpful if you need to be found in an emergency. But the information that you give is extremely useful to the management of the trail.

Quite often someone has swiped all of the pencils at the register. It's a good idea to carry a pen or pencil for a lot of other things, and if you have one with you, you can always sign in. If you find a trail register without a pencil or registration cards, let someone know so that it can be restocked.

TRAILHEAD PARKING

There are many trailhead parking areas noted in the descriptions, in the overall mileage log on pages 32-34, and also on the GPS pages 154–156. These are usually marked with some sort of sign. Sometimes it's just an outline of a backpacker with a "P" under it. It's a good idea to use these lots when you can. Like anyplace else, you should hide any valuables from view, especially if you are going to be on the trail several days. Vandalism has not been much of a problem, but that can happen anywhere to anyone.

Besides these trailhead areas, you can pick up the trail at any of the many forest roads that the trail crosses. See pages 154–156 for GPS coordinates for all of the trailheads and most of the road crossings (most of the major stream crossings too).

ROADS

The OHT begins at the visitor center at Lake Ft. Smith State Park near Mountainburg and Hwy. 71. It crosses Hwys 23, 21, 123, 7, and 65, and currently ends at Hwy. 14, all paved. In between, the OHT crosses many forest roads and gravel county roads. These roads (marked as "FR# 1003" "CR# 5050" etc.) are usually maintained and can be traveled with a normal vehicle. Some are rougher than others so you may need to go slow at times. *Note* that I have maintained the original forest service road numbers on maps, mileage logs, and in the text but will use country road numbers (as "CR# 5050" etc.) too if available— some of these roads have three or four different names, and these names have been known to change from year to year but the forest road numbers will remain the same.

Besides the paved highways and forest roads, there are lots of other roads of all grades scattered along the way. Some are pretty good roads. Others are nothing more than wide trails that used to be roads. I have used many different terms when pointing out a road in the descriptions. Jeep, log, four–wheeler, etc., and many of the terms are interchangeable.

SHUTTLE SERVICES

There are a couple of loops on the OHT, but most of the hiking that is done is one–way. This, of course, requires that you either have two cars and put one at the other end, backtrack on the trail to get back to the car (not such a bad idea, since you will always see something different), or hire a shuttle service.

There are shuttle services—some rent canoes too, and so have the system all set up. In fact, that would make a great trip — to hike part of the trail, like say from Hwy. 23 down to Redding Campground, then get in a canoe and run the Mulberry River. The rates for a shuttle vary greatly, and any of these folks will gladly quote you a price over the phone. And if you are going to do this, I would certainly set it up in advance, instead of showing up there and finding out that they are all booked up. By the way, I have had dealings with all of them, and they are good folks.

TURNER BEND. Located on Hwy. 23 just south of Cass. They also rent canoes, and have *great* sandwiches, plus a general store. Good for shuttles in the western and central parts of the OHT but can go anywhere. 479-667-3641, www.TurnerBend.com.

MOORE OUTDOORS. Located on the Big Piney River near Longpool, good for shuttles on the eastern end of the OHT. Great folks who can also put you on the Big Piney for a great float! 479-331-3606, www.MooreOutdoors.com.

SASSAFRAS SHUTTLE. Ron Ferguson lives near Jasper and can shuttle on the eastern and central sections of the OHT, or even to Lake Ft. Smith State Park if needed (that's a long drive!). 870–446–2910.

BUFFALO RIVER AREA SHUTTLES. For a list of the current concessionaires who are licensed by the National Park Service to offer shuttles, see their web page:
www.nps.gov/buff

TRAIL MILEAGES & GPS

There is a MILEPOST every mile on the trail from 1 to 164 **(no mileposts beyond that yet, including the newest 43.6 miles of the BRT Extension).** The numbers are on carsonite posts that are nailed on trees—see page 1 for an example. They start at Lake Ft. Smith State Park and go east. The mile figure on the post is the mileage back to the state park. I set it up this going west-to-east since the trail is not likely to be extended past the park to the west anytime soon. It is possible that some markers may be missing—let OHTA know if you find any mileposts missing.

I worked long and hard to get the Forest Service to agree to this system. I hope that it is useful to you. Once you get the hang of it, and you use this guide, you can quickly and easily calculate the distance between any two points on the trail. It is just like the mile system used on the Interstates. You can use the mileposts to pace yourself, always know where you are during the day, and figure out how far you've come and how far you've got to go.

At the top of the pages throughout the description sections of this guide you will find mile numbers, like "45.7 — 49.1." This shows the part of the trail that is being described on that particular page. If you are looking for a certain mile, just flip through the guide 'til you find what you are looking for.

2018 update. All of the mileages and milepost locations were recalculated in 2016 using GPS data, and the mileposts were all replaced in 2017-18 by OHTA volunteers (this was required since the new state park location shortened the trail by one mile, also to allow for several trail re-routes that changed distances). All of the text and maps in this guidebook have been updated to match these new numbers and locations. Frequently throughout the descriptive text I will reference the running mileage from Lake Ft. Smith at certain points along the trail. This will correspond with the mileposts, and be shown as a number and fraction—for instance **112.9** would mean milepost 113 will be just ahead. Accuracy for all of the mileages and posts should be within .1.

GPS Something to be aware of—if you use a GPS while hiking (even if using a watch or phone), while they can be very accurate when moving, if you stop along the way the GPS signal continues to move around a little bit seeking an exact location. That means the mileage on the GPS grows even though you are stopped. So if you hike a section of trail that we know is let's say, 4.3 miles, the GPS may actually show it as being longer—sometimes a lot longer (4.4, 4.5, maybe even 5.0 if you stop often!). This can add up during the day to give you a false impression of the miles you hike and how far you have come along the trail. Just sayin'...

MAPS AND ELEVATION PROFILES

All of the maps in this book were created by map maker Ken Eastin of Fayetteville. We feel that the information on these is accurate — let me know anytime that you find out otherwise.

There are no contours on the maps — for many folks that just clutters things up. If you feel the need to have a quad map with you, it takes 15 to cover the original/classic trail route to Woolum (plus several more 43.6 mile extension). The maps for a particular section are listed at the front of that section. For those of you who want to have a copy of all of them, here they are, beginning at the State Park: Mountainburg, Fern, Bidville, Cass, Yale, Oark, Boston, Fallsville, Ozone, Rosetta, Fort Douglas, Sand Gap, Lurton, Moore and Eula. *See info about new maps below.

The *elevation profiles* at the bottom of each map were not designed to be an exact replica of all the ups and downs on the trail. There is just not enough room to do that in this book. They instead show the relative gain or loss of elevation along the route. And since they are tied to many of the major trail points, you can get a good idea of what lies ahead (a big climb, or an easy downhill). Each section begins at zero so you can figure relative to the distance from the beginning.

NEW OHT MAPS. There is a three-map set of very detailed, accurate, and waterproof contour maps with shaded relief in color, and elevation profiles included now available! They also show the milepost locations and other points of interest outside of the trail corridor. The WEST MAP covers the western section from Lake Ft. Smith State Park to Ozone Campground (miles

0.0—84.7). The EAST map covers the eastern section from Ozone to the historic end of the OHT at Woolum (miles 84.7—164.0). The newest NORTH map covers the middle and lower Buffalo River area which now includes 43.6 miles of the Buffalo River Trail that is **also considered part of the OHT. The NORTH map also shows a bushwhack route through the Lower Buffalo Wilderness,** Sylamore Section of the OHT, and rough outline of the future OHT around Lake Norfork to the Missouri Border. Get these maps direct from—www.OzarkHighlandsTrail.com. These maps are a *highly recommended* companion to this guidebook!

TRAIL MARKERS

The OHT is marked with 2 x 6 aluminum blazes — *white* for the main trail, and *blue* for all side and spur trails. **NOTE THAT the OHT/BRT Extension may not be blazed, or at least not as frequently.** They are spaced farther apart than line–of–sight, but not too much. As you hike, you should follow the trail *tread* — don't try to hike from blaze–to–blaze. And any time that you see *two* blazes — one on top of the other, this means that there is a confusing spot ahead. Proceed with caution and look for the next blaze. Also, any time that you see a "leaning" blaze, that means that the trail turns in that direction.

The biggest problem is when the trail runs on a road, and there is a lot of trail on roads. When you are in the woods on trail it's easy to look down and tell that you are on the trail. But when you are on a road, how in the world do you know if the *trail* is still on the road? What you need to do is stay alert and look for the *double* blazes — they will tell you when it's time to turn off.

TRAIL MAINTENANCE

OHTA volunteer members have adopted sections of the trail and do routine maintenance once or twice a year. It is a big job that takes a great deal of work to keep up with (more volunteers are always needed—join OHTA or just participate in a scheduled work trip). But *you* can be a big help too.

First, report any problem areas to the District Office or to OHTA. You can use the mileposts — like, say "There are four large trees down across the trail between milepost #39 and #41." Or "The section of trail to the west of mile #109 really needs some sidehilling." This will help us out a lot. And you too! AND there is now an APP for marking and sending location and condition info to OHTA—see the maintenance section on the OHTA web page for more info (**www.ozarkhighlandstrail.com**).

Something else that you can do is very simple — just kick rocks and small branches off of the trail as you hike it. In fact, you should get into this habit and do it as a natural part of your walking pace, whatever trail you are hiking on. And, of course, you can also adopt a section of trail for yourself. Contact OHTA.

GLOSSARY OF TERMS

Here are a few words that I use over and over again in this guide that you may not be familiar with.

Bench. This is part of a hill, a section that is usually level and runs along the hill for a while. If there was a giant around he could sit on it, like a bench.

FR#/CR#. This is the name of a forest road or county road, and will be followed by a four–digit number, like FR# 1003 or CR# 5050. These are usually gravel roads but sometimes are paved.

Leaf–off. This is the season after all the leaves on the trees fall off, and before they grow new ones in the Spring. There are always a lot more views out through the trees during leaf–off.

Leaf–on. The opposite of leaf–off!

SSS. This means "special scenic spot." There are a lot of places on the trail that may or may not be well known, but are just neat little areas that I find very attractive.

WATERFALL CLASSIFICATIONS

There are many waterfalls along the OHT—mostly flowing only during the wet season (winter and spring), but sometimes they will flow after a good rainfall no matter the season. Some of these are noted in the text, others not. Here is a system that I use to tell how tall a waterfall is, within five or ten feet.

class A — less than five feet tall
class B — five to ten feet tall
class C — ten to fifteen feet tall
class D — more than fifteen feet tall

There are also many other waterfalls near the OHT that may or may not be mentioned. Most of those—plus a couple hundred more—are detailed in my *Arkansas Waterfalls* guidebook.

BUGS

We have all kinds of bugs in Arkansas. Mosquitoes start to come out near the end of April and May. Ticks too. And chiggers like to show up during the summer. And just about the time that they are all getting burned up by the dry weather and heat, horseflies, seed ticks, and gnats come out and really bug you!

There is no surefire way to keep them all from bothering you. A good repellent with DEET will help. Some say soak your clothes in permethrin (then thoroughly dry for a couple of days).

In addition to repellents, a couple of other things will help too. First, don't smell good. Take a shower before you go into the woods, but don't *add* any sweet scents to your body. And campfire smoke really knocks down the bugs. It smells a lot better than perfume anyway. In fact, you might say that campfire smoke is trail perfume!

In August and September, sometimes the spider webs across the trail just drive you nuts. A headnet will usually do the trick, but then of course you don't get as much protein that way — the net will keep you from accidentally eating those fat rascals! This is a good time of the year to hike with a friend — let them lead.

These spiders are often *orb weavers*, with highly seasonal activity. They are fascinating creatures, and were used in the late 60's and early 70's in marijuana research to observe the type of web they wove after getting high. One interesting thing about OWs is they eat their own web in the early mornings! The silk is sort of "recycled" and respun the next day.

If you want to do something neat sometime, get a big piece of white poster board, find a truly magnificent pattern OW web, mist it pretty good with black spray paint, then quickly swing the poster board against it. You end up with a diagram that people really wonder how you managed to draw, because it is so beautiful — makes a great gift for kids.

By late October most of the bugs should be gone 'til spring. Although I have seen ticks out all winter before. And speaking of ticks, I think that many folks are just plain afraid to go into the woods anymore. If you find a tick on you, reach down and pull it off right then. Don't wait. No big deal. Since Lyme disease and other serious diseases are becoming more prevalent, if you suspect a problem, go to a doctor and *tell* him that you've been in the woods and consider ticks as a culprit.

SEASONS

Spring. An excellent time to hike. It's very magical along the OHT in March and April as everything comes to life. There's usually a lot more water too. Of course we've got lots of wildflowers, but the trees flower wildly as well. Especially the dogwoods, redbuds, serviceberry and wild plums.

Summer. It gets pretty hot and muggy towards July and August. Everyone heads to the lakes. You can still find some great hiking if you stick to the areas that have a large stream, and spend your time sitting in it! If you are able to carry enough water, you will probably have the trail to yourself and get in some pretty good hiking. One of my favorite things is getting caught out in a summer thunderstorm.

Fall. Each season has a certain smell to it, but none so nice as the scent of a crisp October day in the woods. Forget about all the blaze of color. Forget the deep blue sky. Forget the craft fairs. Fall just *feels* so good! Pick any part of the trail, and you'll have a great hike. If you are looking for spectacular colors, and there will be lots, try the White Rock or Hare Mtn. areas. It is hard to pinpoint the best week though. You usually can depend on the third and forth weeks of October to be the best.

Winter. This is the longest hiking season on the OHT. Some years we have long stretches of 60–70 degree days, with brilliant sunshine. Much of the trail that runs through an endless tunnel of heavy forest the rest of the year, is now open to the world — with no leaves on the trees you can see deep into the hills and hollows, and out across the countryside. There are no bugs or snakes, and seldom other hikers. Of course it can get down right nasty too! The bottom line here is *be prepared.*

WEATHER

The weather in the Ozarks is just like everywhere else, difficult to predict and constantly changing. Here is a breakdown by month of the type of weather that you are likely to see while on the trail. There are certainly no absolutes, 'cause it is just as likely to be 70 degrees on Christmas Day as it is to be 0. But here are some averages.

January. This is a great month to hike. Lots of nice clear views, and probably some ice formations too. It is one of the coldest months. Daytime highs in the 30's and 40's, with some nice days in the 50's and even 60's. Nighttime lows may be in the teens and twenties, but often down to 0, and once in a while below for a short period. It may snow some, but not too much, and probably won't stay around for long. Rain likely too. But the real killer is an ice storm. They don't happen too often. When they do the forest is just incredible!

February. Expect weather just like January. Possibly a little colder. Witch Hazel bushes will pop open on sunny afternoons along the streams, and the fragrance will soothe the beast in you. I wish that they made a perfume that smelled like this. I'd marry her (actually I did!`).

March. Things are beginning to warm up, and get wetter. Daytime highs in the 50's and 60's, sometimes up into the 70's. Nighttime lows are in the 30's and 40's, with a cold snap into the 20's once in a while. Some snow, but not much. There are often long, soaking rains. Wildflowers begin to pop out. Serviceberry and redbud trees come out and show their colors too.

April. One of the best months of the year. Daytime temps reach into the 70's and even some 80's. The mild nights are in the 40's and 50's, with still a cold snap once in a great while. Sometimes a heavy, wet snow, but this is rare. There can be some great spring thunderstorms. It's a wet month, but lots of sunshine too. Wildflowers are everywhere. And the dogwoods pop out in full bloom, and they are the most common understory tree so it is quite a sight! They will linger around some into May. The rest of the trees begin to green up too. And, as a photographer I notice this, the greens this month are a lot different than at any other time of the year. Don't know why. They just seem to be brighter. And waterfalls are at their peak now. They are everywhere! You will see literally hundreds of them if you hike the entire trail.

May. Another great month, and it is the wettest month of the year. It may rain for days on end. The daytime temps reach into the upper 80's, and the nights seldom get below 60. Wild azaleas are in full bloom now. And there are still lots of wildflowers around. And waterfalls, and more waterfalls. And plenty of sunshine. The trees are all leafed out now.

June. Still good hiking weather. Less rain, and warmer temperatures. The days may reach 90, and it will drop into the 70's at night. This is the last really good month to hike for a while. The bugs start to come out, and the humidity goes up.

July. This is an "iffy" month. It could be cool and wet, but most of the time it is pretty dry and beginning to get hot, up into the 90's, with nights still down into the 70's, or even 60's. When it does rain, it usually does so with lots of power. It's hard to beat spending the afternoon sitting out a summer thunderstorm under a bluff. *But beware.* Arkansas is the fourth leading lightning killer in the country. And I've always heard that an overhang acts like a gap in a spark plug — the lightning jumps this gap and fries whoever is sitting under the bluff! It's also a wonderful experience to hike in the warm rain. Try it sometime.

August. This is a good month to go to the beach or lake. Not a good time to be on the trail. Daytime highs can reach 100, with a humidity reading to match. Sometimes it doesn't get below 80 at night. And there are lots of ticks, chiggers and other assorted bugs just waiting for you. And lots of spider webs strung across the trail. So if you do go hiking, go with someone else taller than you and let them lead (or wear a headnet).

September. This is also a good month to stay home. It is often a worse month than August. Everything is pretty much the same except that horseflies come out, and they are really a pain! Towards the end of the month it does begin to cool off a bit.

October. This is the other best month of the year. The first part of it is usually still quite warm, dry and buggy. But towards the middle the nights get cooler, down into the 50's, 40's and even 30's, and then it frosts. Yet the days are in the 70's and some 80's. By the end of the month it's crisp, clear days and nights, and the forest transforms from the dull green that you have gotten used to since May, into one of the most incredible displays of color anywhere. The last week of the month is always best. The bugs are pretty much gone too. Great hiking weather.

November. Early in the month is still kind of like October. Still some warm days and fall colors. But it can change quickly. The leaves die and fall off of the trees. This turns everything the same color of brown, but also opens up lots of views that have been hidden since April. The days get cooler, down into the 40's and even 30's, with some nice warm days in the 60's. The nights fall into the 20's and 30's more often, and once in a while there will be a cold snap. Rain is more frequent, and once in a great while, some snow. This is the month when hunters are most active — know when the deer season is and wear orange.

December. A good month to hike, believe it or not! The days are usually in the 30's and 40's, but are often in the 50's and above. The nights get cold, and can drop down to zero once in a while. Snow is more likely, but not too much. And it can rain a lot. This is a typical flood month. It is usually pretty dry though, with some rain now and then, and once in a while some ice. The ice begins to accumulate on some of the bluffs and creeks along the trail. A campfire feels great!

CABINS

Lake Ft. Smith State Park is a full-service park with a large visitor center, campsites, and cabin rentals. They are located at the beginning of the OHT right off of Hwy. 71 near Mountainburg. 479–369–2469, www.ArkansasStateParks.com.

White Rock Mountain is located at mile 18.7 on the OHT and has three rustic stone cabins plus a lodge building for rent (the best view on the entire trail!). They also have a campground and hiker shuttles. 479–369–4128, www.WhiteRockMountain.com.

Buffalo River Area. There are many—google is your friend...

EMERGENCIES

If you have cell service (or sometimes not), **DIAL 911.**

I have always hiked alone most of the time, and have more or less decided that if anything serious ever happened to me, well, then I would either make it home or I would end my life in one of the most beautiful places in the world. When there are other people involved, then you have to start thinking about what to do and how to get help if something goes wrong.

It's always a good idea to have either this guide or a map with you when you are on the OHT (or both). If you do have a problem and have to get to help in a hurry, you may be able to tell where you are and find a road that will get you to help. This is a remote trail. You won't find too many houses nearby, but you will always be within a few miles of a forest road.

These days I always carry a PERSONAL TRACKER/LOCATOR with me—the current popular ones are made by InReach and Find Me Spot. While it is possible to actually upload your location to a map on a web page while you hike along, I use mine to send a "checking in and OK" e-mail once in a while to let my bride know where I am. Most importantly these have a

911 button to push if you get in a real life-threatening emergency that sends a signal via satellites that will begin a full-blown search and rescue mission to find you. This could save your life if you are in grave danger, but casual or accidental use could also trigger an unwarranted rescue mission that could potentially cost you thousands of dollars—so KNOW HOW TO USE ONE, and be very careful when and how you use one.

If you are totally lost and don't have a personal locator or cell phone and/or signal to call for help, don't despair. The best thing to do is get comfortable, make yourself at home, start a fire, and wait. The main thing is to not panic. Panic kills. So you end up spending a day or two in the woods that you hadn't counted on. It just might be the best thing that has happened to you in a while. Remember, stay calm. You'll be all right. And stay put. If you left word with someone where you were hiking and when to expect you to be back, and you faithfully signed in at all the trail registers you came to, someone will most like come find you.

CELL SERVICE

There is more cell service available along the OHT all the time, but it is not a given anywhere. There is *no* service along much of the trail so *don't count on a signal.* Service is best on the ridgetops and worst in the valleys. These days I use a satellite messenger for texts and even email from almost anywhere along the trail. My bride won't let me leave home without one!

 One last note. Near the front of each description section, you will find the hiker symbol — this is the beginning point for the description of that section.

And I have included several tips about various things here and there that you might like to know about — these "*barefoot notes*" are marked with bare feet.

Thanks for spending time with me reading this guide. I hope that it is useful to you, that you have many safe and enjoyable hikes on the OHT, and that I get to see ya in the woods someday...

Tim
Tim Ernst

TRAIL MILEAGE LOG (continuous trail 207.6 miles)

Here are mileages along the main/continuous stretch of the OHT going both directions (Lake Ft. Smith to Dillards Ferry, 207.6 miles). Descriptions of the trail sections are written from WEST to EAST. Mile points are measured from the west end at Lake Ft. Smith Park to current east end at Dillards Ferry.

Trail Point	Mile Point and Mileage West to East	Mileage East to West
Lake Ft. Smith State Park	0.0	207.6
Frog Bayou Creek west side	2.9	204.7
Forest Service boundary at Jack Creek	5.4	202.2
Jack Creek	8.3	199.3
Dockerys Gap Trailhead/FR# 1007	9.3	198.3
Hurricane Creek	10.0	197.6
FR# 1703	13.2	194.4
FR# 1003/1505	15.1	192.5
Spur trail to Shores Lake West Loop	16.6	191.0
Shores Lake Trailhead (spur)	21.4	195.8
Spur trail to White Rock	17.4	190.2
White Rock Mtn. Trailhead (spur)	17.7	190.5
Spur trail to Shores Lake East Loop	19.0	188.6
Salt Fork Creek	19.2	188.4
Potato Knob Mtn./FR# 1510	21.3	186.3
Spirits Creek	23.6	184.0
Ragtown Road/FR# 1509	24.8	182.8
Railroad Bed — west end	26.1	181.5
Railroad Bed — east end	28.8	178.8
Fane Creek	30.3	177.3
Whiting Mountain	34.0	173.6
Rock House	35.2	172.4
Cherry Bend Trailhead/Hwy. 23	35.5	172.1
East Fly Gap Rd./FR# 1503	39.1	168.5
Hare Mountain	41.3	166.3
Hare Mountain Trailhead	43.1	164.5
Redding/Spy Rock Spur	45.1	162.5
Redding Campground (spur)	49.5	(spur) 166.9
Herrods Creek	46.2	161.4
Indian Creek	50.0	157.6
Spur Trail To Indian Creek Trailhead	50.9	156.7
Indian Creek Trailhead (spur)	51.6	(spur) 157.4
Briar Branch	52.5	155.1
Lick Branch Trailhead/CR# 5051	55.1	152.5
Little Mulberry Creek/CR# 5099	56.9	150.7
FR# 1453/CR# 6200	64.7	142.9
Lynn Hollow Creek	69.1	138.5
Arbaugh Road Trailhead/FR# 1404	70.0	137.6
Lewis Prong Creek, west	72.0	135.6
Lewis Prong Creek, east	74.4	133.2

Trail Point	Mile Point and Mileage West to East	Mileage East to West
Waterfall Hollow Creek	77.0	130.6
Moonhull Mountain	77.5	130.1
Boomer Branch	81.0	126.6
Mulberry River	83.3	124.3
FR# 1003/CR# 5440	83.4	124.2
Ozone Trailhead/Hwy. 21	84.7	122.9
Little Piney River	87.0	120.6
FR# 1405/CR# 5550	88.3	119.3
Owens Creek	89.6	118.0
Lick Creek	92.3	115.3
FR# 1004/CR# 5671 Trailhead	94.3	113.3
Cedar Creek	96.5	111.1
Cedar Creek Pool	96.7	110.9
FR# 1003/CR# 5680 Trailhead	97.9	109.7
Gee Creek	100.6	107.0
Hwy. 123	102.1	105.5
Haw Creek Falls Campground	102.4	105.2
Ft. Douglas/Big Piney TH/Hwy 123	103.8	103.8
Hurricane Creek Wilderness (enter)	104.1	103.5
Bypass Trail	107.8	99.8
Hurricane Creek, west	109.4	98.2
Natural Bridge	109.9	97.7
Greasy Creek	112.0	95.6
Hurricane Creek, east	113.4	94.2
Spur Trail to Chancel Trailhead	117.1	90.5
Chancel Trailhead (spur)	117.7	(spur) 91.2
Hurricane Creek Wilderness (leave)	117.4	90.2
Unnamed Creek	119.5	88.1
4-wheeler road/Buck Branch	121.8	85.8
Fairview Trailhead/Hwy. 7	**123.8**	**83.8**
FR# 1255/CR# 5000	126.1	81.5
Cox Hollow	127.6	80.0
Greenhaw Hollow	129.3	78.3
Unnamed Hollow	130.4	77.2
Moore CCC Camp/Spur to TH	133.0	74.6
Moore CCC Trailhead (spur)	**133.6**	(spur) **75.2**
Richland Creek crossing #1	133.2	74.4
Ben Hur/Moore Trailhead	**134.5**	**73.1**
FR# 1203/CR# 5050	135.0	72.6
Falling Water Creek	138.4	69.2
Richland Creek Campground TH	**143.1**	**64.5**
Long Branch	145.4	62.2
Armstrong Hollow	147.5	60.1
Stack Rock Trailhead/FR# 1201	**150.8**	**56.8**
Dry Creek	152.9	54.7
National Forest Boundary	155.6	52.0
Buffalo River at Woolum	**164.0**	**43.6**

(continues on next page)

Trail Point	Mile Point and Mileage West to East	Mileage East to West
Richland Creek crossing #3	164.2	43.4
Point Peter Mountain	165.2	42.4
Ben Branch	167.5	40.1
Dave Manes Bluff	168.0	39.6
Hage Hollow Creek	170.1	37.5
Whisenant Hollow Bluffs	171.3	36.3
Tie Slide	173.2	34.4
Calf Creek	176.3	31.3
Collier Homestead Trailhead	**177.1**	**30.5**
Tyler Bend VC (via spur)	178.5	29.9
Grinders Ferry TH/Hwy. 65	**179.0**	**28.6**
Long Bottom Road	180.6	27.0
Illinois Point	180.9	26.7
Amphitheater Falls	181.7	25.9
Gilbert Overlook	183.1	24.5
Bear Creek	184.8	22.8
Zack Ridge Road Trailhead	**185.6**	**22.0**
Brush Creek	186.7	20.9
Red Bluff Spur Trail	187.5	20.1
Red Bluff Road Trailhead	**190.1**	**17.5**
Rocky Creek	192.0	15.6
Little Rocky Creek	193.3	14.3
Pileated Point	193.5	14.1
Hoot-Owl Hollow	194.7	12.9
Saw-Whet Owl Falls	195.0	12.6
South Maumee Road Trailhead	**196.3**	**11.3**
Maumee Falls East	197.2	10.4
Spring Creek	199.6	8.0
CR#99 (Spring Creek Road)	201.6	6.0
Kimball Creek	205.0	2.6
Dillards Ferry/Hwy. 14	**207.6**	**0.0**

(this is the current western end of continuous trail as of 2022)

THE TRAIL CONTINUES, WITH GAPS

LOWER BUFFALO RIVER WILDERNESS BUSHWHACK*
(no trail, bushwhack only, awaiting NPS approval)   16–20 mile gap

SYLAMORE SECTION OF THE OHT, 31.6 miles
  (map and hiking descriptions begin on page 140)

Spring Creek Road/Trailhead	**0.0**
Cross Spring Creek	7.9
Moccasin Spring Trailhead/Hwy. 341 (1st cross)	**9.0**
Barkshed Road	12.4
Cripple Turkey Trailhead (Jct. N. Sylamore Trail)	**13.9**
Cole Fork	14.3
Brush Creek Trailhead/Hwy. 341 (2nd cross)	**18.1**
Hwy. 341—3rd crossing	22.4
Hwy. 341—4th crossing	29.6
Matney Knob Trailhead/Hwy. 341	**31.6**

Matney Knob Trailhead/Hwy. 341 to Lake Norfork Dam 8.0 gap
(no trail, all state highway or county road)

LAKE NORFORK SECTIONS (OHT, Ozark Keystone/David's Trail)

Lake Norfork from Damsite Trailhead (completed)	**13.0**
Lake Norfork OKT section **(under construction)**	25.0 gap
Lake Norfork OKT /David's Trail (completed)	17.0
Lake Norfork OKT to Missouri border **(under construction)** 7.0 gap	

---

*The Lower Buffalo River section of the route is 16–20 miles long but exists
in 2021 as a bushwhack route only and not official constructed trail (waiting
on NPS approval and exact route location). From the end of constructed trail
at Dillards Ferry/Hwy. 14, this bushwhack route continues east/downstream
along the Buffalo National River and passes through the Lower Buffalo
Wilderness Area.

   The general route has been documented in at least two publications for
hikers to follow using map and compass, GPS, etc.—
   Ozark Highlands Trail NORTH map by Underwood Geographics
   Hiker's Guide, OHT Route, Lower Buffalo Wilderness by Duane Woltjen
Both are available for sale from the OHTA website online store
(www.OzarkHighlandsTrail.com)

MY GOAL for the next update to this guidebook (#8) will be to
include descriptions, maps, and mileages for all of the missing
miles/gaps above in Arkansas to the Missouri border.

SECTION ONE — 17.7 miles
Lake Ft. Smith State Park to White Rock Mountain

Trail Point	Mile Point	Mileage West–East	Mileage East–West
Lake Ft. Smith State Park	0.0	0.0	17.7
Frog Bayou Creek (west side)	2.9	2.9	14.8
Ozark Nat'l. Forest boundary	5.4	5.4	12.3
Jack Creek	8.3	8.3	9.4
Dockerys Gap/FR# 1007	9.3	9.3	8.4
Hurricane Creek	10.0	10.0	7.7
Pipeline	11.6	11.6	6.1
FR# 1703	13.2	13.2	4.5
Woods Gap/FR#1003/1505	15.1	15.1	2.6
Shores Lake Loop Trail West	16.6	16.6	1.1
Spur trail to White Rock	17.4	17.4	.3
White Rock Mountain TH	17.4 +.3 spur	17.7	0.0

The OHT begins at the Lake Ft. Smith State Park. Both the park and first 5.3 miles of the trail were opened to the public in late 2007 after having been closed for five years to create a new, larger lake for water supply. There used to be two lakes here—Lake Ft. Smith and Lake Shepherd Springs, but a new dam was built where the old state park (and previous beginning of the OHT) used to be. There is a visitor center at the new park, along with campgrounds, cabin rentals, interpretive facilities and events, and it is a fitting home for the beginning of the OHT.

The park is located just off of Hwy. 71 (Boston Mountain Scenic Loop) a few miles north of Mountainburg—take the 34 exit on I-49, then take Hwy. 282 to Hwy. 71, then turn left onto Hwy. 71, and finally turn right after 4.2 miles onto a paved county road (just south of the famous Artist Point, a great sunrise spot) that will take you on down the hill two miles to the visitor center, which will be on your right. There is a special section at the visitor center to park for the OHT, and check in with park service staff there if you will be leaving your vehicle overnight. Fern and Bidville quad maps. 35.69578° N, -94.11925° W

*CAUTION: There probably will not be a bridge across Frog Bayou Creek at mile 2.9. When water levels are high in the creek this can be a **dangerous crossing**. Check with the park if you think water levels*

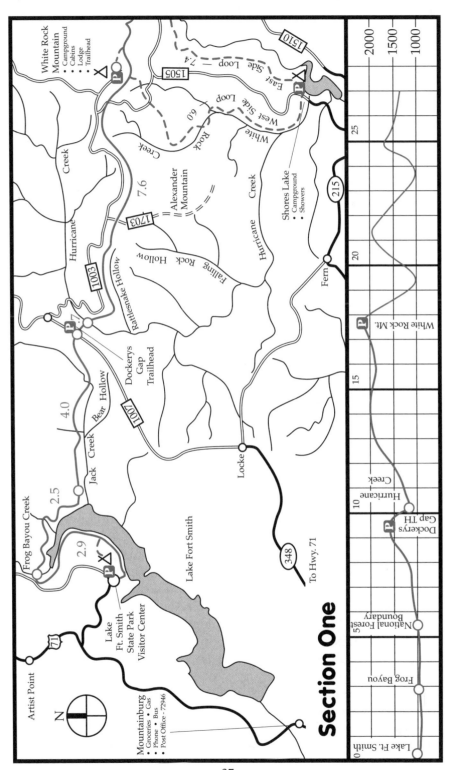

White Rock Mountain
- Campground
- Cabins
- Lodge
- Trailhead

1510

East Side Loop — 7.4

1505

West Side Loop
6.0

White Rock Creek

Alexander Mountain

1703

7.6

Creek

Hurricane Creek

Shores Lake
- Campground
- Showers

215

Fern

1003

Falling Rock Hollow

Rattlesnake Hollow

Hurricane Creek

White Rock Mt.

P.7

Dockerys Gap Trailhead

1007

Bear Hollow

4.0

Jack Creek

2.5

Locke

Frog Bayou Creek

2.9

348

To Hwy. 71

Lake Fort Smith

71

Artist Point

Lake Ft. Smith State Park Visitor Center

N

Mountainburg
- Groceries • Gas
- Phone • Bus
- Post Office - 72946

Section One

2000

1500

1000

25

20

White Rock Mt.

15

Hurricane Creek

10

Dockerys Gap TH

National Forest Boundary

5

Frog Bayou

Lake Ft. Smith

0

might be high before you begin or end your hike at Lake Ft. Smith State Park (479–369–2469). Options include taking a boat across the lake, or starting/ending your hike at Dockerys Gap, mile 9.3.

The trail begins at the visitor center—on the left hand side if you are facing the front of the building. The trail takes off down the hill towards the lake, and soon comes to an overlook where you have a grand SSS view of the lake spread out before you. From the overlook the trail heads out to the left and enters the woods. It is marked with 2" x 6" white blazes. Trees may also be marked with other colors of blazes to signify other trails, but you want to stick with the white blazes.

For the first couple of miles the trail remains fairly level and just inside the treeline, with the lake visible during leaf-off out to your right. It does some up and downing and it works across several small drainages. There are some rocky areas along with wide open forest. The first part of this section runs just below part of the campground, but eventually the trail gets through the main part of the park and into the general forest area, with the lake remaining a constant companion out to the right.

The trail eases away from the lake and uphill just a little bit, then passes a spur trail that goes up to the left and back to the campground—continue STRAIGHT AHEAD. There is a nice SSS waterfall just beyond at .9. From the waterfall the trail dips down and through another rocky drainage, then bumps up a little bit, then slips on down below the hillside and back towards the lake once again, passing through an old homesite area at 1.0 (sinkhole/old well on the right).

Before long the trail comes alongside a small bluff on the left, and the trail continues along the base of this bluff for a little bit, getting pretty close to the lake. In fact the bluff, big trees, and giant block boulders you will see now and then, plus great views up and down the lake, I would list this whole area as an SSS!

The trail remains down near the lake to 1.6 and comes to the first of two old homesite areas and a rock chimney next to the trail—a great homesite location!. Soon after the first chimney you will come to Shepherd Spring, and the stone cistern that was constructed around the spring to contain the water at 1.8. There is some pretty nice rock work at the back of this—a historical SSS. From the spring the trail continues along near the lake, passing the second chimney and homestead area. If you look across the lake you can see the Jack Creek Drainage, which is where you will be headed once on the other side of the lake.

At 1.9 the trail joins an old road/four-wheeler trail—TURN LEFT onto the road. Follow this road as it curves back to the left and runs along just above Frog Bayou Creek, which you can see down to your right. The trail route leaves the old roadbed at one point up to the left to avoid a spot where Frog Bayou has eroded the roadbed away, then rejoins the roadbed. And just beyond that point, at 2.8, just *before* the road/trail intersects with a main county road coming down from the left, TURN RIGHT (at the large boulders that are blocking the trail), and DO NOT join the county road. The trail will take you down across a *small* side creek, then veer to the right and over to Frog Bayou Creek at 2.9 (there may be some confusion here so watch for blazes).

The trail will cross Frog Bayou Creek on an angle to the left— look to the other side of the creek upstream a bit to see where the trail continues. *Note:* the creek changes course sometimes and so you may have to cross the creek in two or sometimes in three sections. You will probably have to wade at least one of the crossings, perhaps all of them. *CAUTION—these may be dangerous crossings if the water is high, and it is never a good idea to cross flowing water that you can't see the bottom of! So please, if the water is high and/or muddy, turn back.*

In between crossings the trail runs for a short distance through a thick forest to the last crossing at 3.0. Once on the other side of this last crossing the trail heads up into the woods to the right through a very rocky area. If you look UP you may spot a nice bluff, which is one of the largest in the area. The trail works up onto the first bench above the creek valley and passes through an old homesite area. From that point for the next couple of miles the trail remains mostly level, curving out towards the outside edge of the bench (some really nice SSS views), then working back into the hillside and dips down a little bit to cross a drainage, then back out towards the outside edge of the bench once again. There is a nice SSS creek at 4.2. If the water is running well this is a good spot to stop and explore upstream if you have the time.

The trail continues mostly on the level with a bit of up and downing as it works into and out of small drainages, to 4.8, where you will get your last view down the lake before leaving the lake area for good. From that point the trail leaves the hillside, drops on down to the bottomlands and curves

back to the left into the Jack Creek drainage and goes across a
four-wheeler road at 5.0. The trail comes alongside Jacks Creek
for a little bit, then veers away and passes the national forest
boundary at 5.4.

The trail climbs up a short distance onto a bench that looks
down onto Jack Creek, and stays there, doing a little up–and–
downing. It crosses several creeks and past 6.0. There are some
nice camp spots in between these creeks.

Continuing on the same general bench, the trail goes through
a neat rocky area, and eventually drops on down off the hill into
the bottom. If you were to hike across this bottom land, and cross
Jack Creek, you'd come to Bear Branch, a nice little creek area
with several waterfalls in it.

The trail runs along in the bottom for a short distance, curves
around to the left, then the right, and crosses a creek. There is
often a horse packer's camp in this area. It bumps up over a
small rise, then back down again, then runs level a while.

It climbs up a little bit past 7.0, as it continues along another
bench. It eventually drops down to and crosses a small stream.
This stream has an almost house–sized boulder plopped right
down into the middle of it. At 7.4 the trail crosses another creek.
Just upstream from the trail is a "slough" area that is worth a
look.

Right after the creek crossing, the trail hits an old road,
TURNS RIGHT here, and follows the road. A couple of hundred
yards later the trail TURNS LEFT off of the road, back into the
woods. It's pretty easy hiking for a while, and the trail passes 8.0.
From here the trail goes uphill a little, then downhill into the Jack
Creek bottom once again, makes a sharp turn to the right, then
crosses Jack Creek, in two sections at 8.2.

Cross the first part of the creek, then turn a little to the left
and cross the second, main part of the creek. Cross the jeep road
on the other side and continue on trail into the woods. It follows
beside the road for a short distance, crossing another jeep road,
then turns to the right, and follows a small creek upstream.

If you need a rest here, follow this small stream downstream
(across jeep road) to Jack Creek. There is a wonderful area on
Jack Creek just upstream — an SSS. Back on the trail, it follows
the small stream for a little ways, then crosses it and begins the
climb out of the Jack Creek drainage. The trail climbs up, turns
back to the left, then the right, then uphill some more through a

real rocky area. At 8.6 the trail passes under a giant boulder. One more switchback and some more rocky terrain, then the trail tops out and levels off.

On the level, the trail passes 9.0. It continues on the level, and joins an old road. This road eventually hits another old road, BEAR RIGHT at this intersection, staying on the road. A short distance later the trail crosses FR# 1007 at 9.2. This road is also called the Locke Road, as the community of Locke is several miles down the road to the south. Back to the north is Dockerys Gap. Also to the north a couple hundred feet is a trailhead parking area.

Cross the forest road and head into the woods on trail. It drops on down the hill, past a trail register and spur trail to trailhead, turns sharp right, and then begins a really steep descent. This is not a fun climb if going in the other direction! It switchbacks down the hill, dropping into the Hurricane Creek Valley. Once in the bottom, the trail crosses a jeep road, and then Hurricane Creek at 10.0.

This crossing is always a wet one, and during high water can be a little dangerous. If you prefer to cross dry and have the time, there is a way around it. Go back a few feet to the jeep road and follow it upstream. It's a third of a mile to a forest road and a bridge. Cross the creek there, then go back downstream to the trail crossing.

Hurricane Creek is the *last reliable water source* until White Rock, so fill up if you need to! Just across Hurricane Creek, the trail turns left (upstream) for a short ways, then turns uphill and to the right. It makes its way up several benches, then levels off along the edge of a bench, looking down on the creek. There are some great views along this section, especially during leaf–off.

The trail continues its uphill pace — up a bench or two, then level for a while, then back uphill again. You are in the middle of an 800 foot elevation gain, through a nice boulder/bluff area that is worth some exploration time if you have it , and past 11.0. The drainage off to the right is a rather confusing one. I have two maps that show two names for it. One is Devil's Hollow, the other says that it is Rattlesnake Hollow. Both maps show the other hollow to be the next one to the south! (I'm satisfied now that it is Rattlesnake Hollow—and Rattlesnake Falls!).

 . The trail continues uphill, a bench at a time. It crosses a natural gas pipeline at 11.6, makes a little turn in the woods beyond, then begins a rather steep climb up the nose of a ridge. The pipeline takes natural gas from the National Forest area up into southern Missouri. This is certainly one of the reasons that we have National Forest lands, to produce gas, oil, timber, AND recreation such as the OHT. It is nice that we can all survive together.

There are some nice rock formations on this climb, and the views are great during leaf–off. Once you level off, that is about it for climbing for a while! Out in the level woods the trail passes 12.0, and then crosses a jeep trail at 12.3. If you need water here you might check down this road to the right a couple hundred feet — the headwaters of Devil's / Rattlesnake Hollow creek is here, and often has water in it. There are several gas wells (feeding the pipeline) down this road too.

Continue across the jeep road, up a slight hill, then down a little on the other side. The trail crosses a small creek that has water in it about half of the year. There is a wonderful view down into Falling Rock Hollow, and this is another one of my SSS's. At this point you are on Richason Mountain, and pass 13.0.

From about the pipeline to White Rock, the trail is always within a couple of hundred yards of FR# 1003, which is the main road that crosses the Forest. This is where you should go if an emergency comes up while in this area.

From 13.0 the trail continues level, then bumps up to and across FR# 1703 (dead end) at 13.2. It continues out into the woods, rises up just a little, runs level, then drops off, and begins somewhat of a descent, one bench at a time. During leaf–off, you get your first view of White Rock Mountain in this area.

The trail runs along an old, narrow pioneer road for a while, and just as it gets to the bottom of a short descent on this old road, it passes 14.0. There are some nice, large trees and some neat boulder areas all through here. More large rocks, and lots of giant trees.

As the trail breaks out of this area and drops down a little, it passes 15.0, then just beyond, at 15.1, the trail crosses FR# 1003 at Woods Gap. The trail continues into the woods on the other side of the road. If you turned right on the road, it would take you to Shores Lake. Turn left, then right and you will end up at White Rock. Staying on the trail, it heads uphill just a little, goes over a large slab rock, then intersects with a jeep road. TURN RIGHT on this road and follow it downhill.

The trail continues on this road, as it works its way down and then around underneath the bluffs up on White Rock. You can look up and see the bluff area from this road. Still on the old road, the trail passes 16.0. From here the road loops around the ridge that comes down from the main pavilion up on White Rock, and then comes to a trail intersection at 16.6.

The main trail continues STRAIGHT AHEAD (or to the left). The trail to the right goes on down to Shores Lake (blue blazes), and is part of a 14.4–mile loop. The map and description of that loop trail can be found on page 144. One problem that the Forest Service has with trail signs in this area is that the bears in the area like to eat them. Hum.

From this intersection, the trail continues on around the hill on the old road. As you start down a slight hill there is a great view of the bluffs above. The road disappears, and the trail drops down, crosses a small stream, then works its way up a little on the other side.

The trail comes up and around a small hill past 17.0, then remains fairly level, with some ups and downs, but nothing too serious. Eventually, it works its way up a little steeper, and up to another trail intersection at 17.4. The main trail turns right, and heads down into Salt Fork Creek. TURN LEFT and continue up to White Rock Mountain (blue blazes).

The trail rises a little, comes alongside the lower part of a bluffline, and to a trail register. *Be sure and register*, even if you already have. We need lots of names on those cards! From the register, the trail actually goes under the bluff for a short distance. There is probably enough room to get in out of the rain. Then it heads up, and turns right, up through the bluffline.

Once on top there is a lesser trail to the right — this will take you to the easternmost point of the bluff (good for sunrises). TURN LEFT and follow the main trail along the ridgetop. There is another trail that takes off to the left in a short distance — this trail actually makes a loop all the way around the mountain and ends up in the same place — see pages 148–149 for description and map.

The main trail continues on the ridgetop and comes out on a dead end road next to a cabin at 17.7. You have arrived at White Rock! Follow the road. There are three cabins and a lodge building on the left. The trailhead parking area is on the right just in front of the second cabin. To get to the campground, continue on this road. It will turn right in front of the lodge, swing past the caretaker's house (there is an emergency phone there), then turn left a couple of hundred feet beyond into the campground.

This is a pretty basic campground. There are eight sites plus an overflow area, pit toilets and water (in season). There is a fee. There is a little trail that heads down into the woods to the west and comes out on the bluff for that great view.

The cabins and the lodge building were built by the Civilian Conservation Corps back in the 1930's. They were built to last a long time, like most of the buildings that they built. The buildings, in bad shape and getting worse, were slated to be destroyed when members of the Ozark Highlands Trail Association joined hands with others to save them. "The Friends of White Rock" organization was formed in 1987 and a campaign was begun to fix them up. Close to $100,000 in materials, labor, cash donations and grants was raised to do the job.

There is room for 28 folks to spend the night in the lodge, in bunkbeds. It has a stove, sink, showers, toilets and a refrigerator. There is also a separate room in the basement that is reserved especially for hikers — call and ask about reserving it before your hike. The cabins and lodge are open all year. This is a really special place to spend some time! To get more information, and to reserve a cabin, call 479–369–4128.

The most spectacular view in this part of the country is just to the west of the lodge building. There is a picnic area there (no camping), with a trail that leads down to the main pavilion on the point. There is a long bluffline here that is the best spot to watch the sunset. It is great here at any time of the year. And there is no finer spot anywhere to view the fall colors during late October. It's definitely one of my SSS's, as well as one of my favorite spots anywhere. The elevation is 2280 feet.

A word of caution here. There have been a number of folks who have fallen off of the bluffs here and have been seriously hurt or killed. This is not a place for young children, or drunks. In fact, because of all the accidents, the bluff area is officially closed from sunset until sunrise. Please be careful!

The loop trail around the mountain is not marked, but since it simply follows along on top of the bluff, it's easy to find (see page 148). And there are four wood pavilions along it. The view from the entire trail is unequalled. There was once a fire lookout tower here — it is now an observation tower on a military range in Oklahoma. The stone tower that still exists is actually a water tower.

There are many ways to get to White Rock (at least nine that I know of), and all of them involve dirt road. RV's are not recommended. Here is the way with the *least* amount of dirt roads: Take exit #24 off of Interstate 40, go north on Hwy. 215 past the community of Fern, continue on 215 about three more miles to FR# 1505 (Shores Lake Road, paved) — turn left here at the sign and go just over one mile to Shores Lake (the pavement ends here and it becomes Bliss Ridge Road). Continue past the lake area on dirt road to FR# 1003 (White Rock Mtn. Road) — turn left here, then go 2.2 miles and turn right at the next intersection (FR# 1505/Hurricane Road), then bear right at the next intersection (that will take you past the carved entrance rock), and follow the road on up the hill and into the White Rock Recreation Area. GPS 35.68953° N -93.95447° W

There is a detailed map of this area on page 149.

If you build a campfire, always sit uphill from it in the evening, and downhill in the morning. This is because the wind will **usually** *settle at the end of the day as it cools (taking the campfire smoke with it), and rise in the morning as it warms. If you are near a creek, sit upstream at night and downstream in the morning.*

SECTION TWO — 18.4 miles
White Rock Mountain to Cherry Bend Trailhead/Hwy.23

Trail Point	Mile Point	Mileage West–East	Mileage East–West
White Rock Mountain TH	17.4 +.3 spur	0.0	18.4
Main Trail Intersection	17.4	.3	18.1
Shores Lake Loop Trail East	19.0	1.9	16.5
Salt Fork Creek	19.2	2.1	16.3
Potato Knob Mtn./FR#1510	21.3	4.2	14.2
Spirits Creek	23.6	6.5	11.9
Ragtown Road/FR# 1509	24.8	7.7	10.7
Railroad Bed — begin	26.1	9.0	9.4
Railroad Bed — end	28.8	11.7	6.7
Fane Creek	30.3	13.2	5.2
Whiting Mountain	34.0	16.9	1.5
Rock House	35.2	18.1	.3
Spur trail to Cherry Bend	35.4	18.3	0.1
Cherry Bend TH/Hwy. 23	35.4 + .1 spur	18.4	0.0

This 18.4 mile section begins at one of the most popular spots on the OHT, and one of the prettiest areas in the state, White Rock Mountain (see page 148 for a complete description of this area and how to get there, also page 149 for a detailed map). This section is all on the Boston Mountain Ranger District. The trail sort of roller–coasters up and down the ridges as it heads east. Spirits Creek is certainly a highlight, as well as the historical railroad bed. And there is an unusual rockhouse shelter just before this section ends at Hwy. 23.

To get to the trailhead at White Rock by road, continue straight past the campground as you enter the recreation area, past the caretaker's house, then bear left just beyond (the right fork in the road leads to a picnic area). This road leads past the lodge and three cabins before it dead ends. The trailhead parking area is in front of the middle cabin and on the left. The trail takes off from the end of the road in front of the last cabin. For cabin reservations — 479–369–4128. Quad maps are Bidville and Cass. GPS 35.68953° N, -93.95447° W

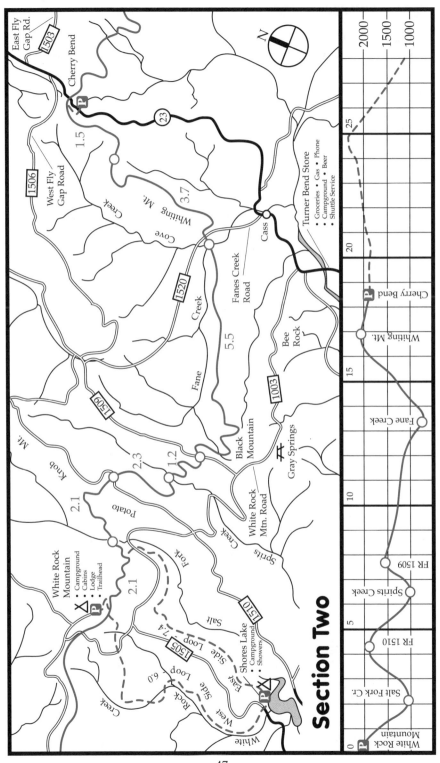

Section Two

East Fly
Gap Rd.
1503

Cherry Bend

23

1.5

1506

West Fly
Gap Road

3.7

Whiting Mt.

Cove Creek

Creek

1520

5.5

Fanes Creek
Road

Cass

Turner Bend Store
• Groceries • Gas • Phone
• Campground • Beer
• Shuttle Service

Fane Creek

Bee
Rock

1003

1509

Black
Mountain

2.3

1.2

White Rock
Mtn. Road

Gray Springs

Knob Mt.

2.1

Potato

Spirts Creek

White Rock
Mountain
△ Campground
□ Cabins
• • • Lodge
• • • Trailhead

2.1

Fork

Salt

1510

1505

East Side Loop

7.4

Shores Lake
• Campground
• Showers

6.0

West Side Loop

White Rock Creek

47

The trail starts off down the top of a small ridge. This first short section is marked with blue blazes. A lesser trail intersects from the right — this is a loop trail that goes all the way around the top of the mountain (described on page 148). Continue straight ahead, then TURN RIGHT at the second intersection. A lesser trail goes straight, and on around the mountain.

The trail drops down through the bluffline, TURNING LEFT about half way down. It levels off under the bluff where you will come to a trail register. *Please sign in.* It then continues down the hill, and winds around to the main trail intersection at 17.3, which should be signed. The right fork goes to Shores Lake and Lake Ft. Smith. TURN LEFT here and continue down the ridge. This is marked with white blazes.

The trail works its way down the ridge, past some giant old hardwoods, down to an old road. A couple hundred feet later TURN LEFT off of the road. You will continue heading down, one bench at a time, cross a couple of jeep roads and a small stream, across a flat area, then intersect with another jeep road. TURN LEFT on the road. It forks about fifty feet later — TURN RIGHT here, still on the road. It heads downhill rather steeply at this point. If you look across the valley out in front of you, you will see Potato Knob Mountain. The trail will eventually climb up there and cross over in the saddle between the two knobs. Be alert while you are on this road for four–wheelers zooming past.

This road takes you down two benches, then TURNS LEFT off of the road and out into the woods. The trail runs level for a while, crosses a small stream, then turns right and heads down the hill again. It drops down several benches and come to a trail intersection at 19.0 — this is where the east side of the Shores Lake to White Rock Loop continues on (see page 144 for map and description). It is 5.4 miles down to Shores Lake, and is blazed with blue. Just beyond that intersection, the main OHT hits a jeep road — TURN LEFT here and stay on the road for about a hundred yards, and TURN LEFT again off of the road. You are now in the bottom of the drainage. There is a nice camping spot here, although it would be better if you could get off the trail.

Salt Fork Creek is just ahead at 19.2. You can usually find a dry crossing here, though you may have to look a little. If the water is dangerously high, hike downstream about a half mile and cross on a forest road bridge, then follow a jeep road back upstream to the trail.

The trail goes straight across the creek and a jeep road on the other side, then heads up into the woods. It works its way up, bench after bench, sometimes at rather steep pitches for a short distance. After each climb, be sure and turn around and enjoy the view as you catch your breath. There are some nice rock formations too. The trail climbs up further, and eventually works its way alongside a stream, making its way up the hill next to it, and past 20.0. There is a class B waterfall in this area. Soon after, you level off, cross a jeep road, and then you cross the stream that you've been following. There may not be any more water 'til Spirits Creek at 23.5, so fill up if you need to.

From the creek the trail is not nearly as steep, as it winds out through the woods. It climbs up a little and crosses the same creek again, near another class B falls, and eventually tops out on a level bench. Here it intersects with an old road. TURN RIGHT on this road, as it runs on the level.

This is a nice little section of easy walking through 21.0 and past another small stream. And just beyond this, TURN LEFT off of the road and head slightly uphill into the woods. This will take you up next to and down below a forest road. The trail then swings to the left, and finally climbs up to and across FR# 1510 at 21.3. This is the saddle of Potato Knob Mountain that I spoke of.

Go straight across the road and down the other side of the hill. The trail swings to the left and drops down to and intersects with a jeep road. TURN RIGHT on the road. It continues to head downhill, then levels off and makes a sharp left turn. At this turn there are two other roads that turn right. TURN RIGHT ON THE SECOND ROAD, and stay on it (the first road goes uphill, the road that you want stays level). Unfortunately, there are a number of four–wheeler trails and jeep roads in this section that we intersect with. You need to stay alert when on these roads and watch for the trail to leave them — all of these spots are blazed with double blazes.

About a quarter mile down this road another road/trail comes in from the left — GO STRAIGHT and stay on the road. This is a nice easy hiking section and basically level past 22.0. And just about the time that you begin to snooze, the trail TURNS LEFT off of this road, and heads down into the woods.

It works its way down through a rocky bench, and lands on another four–wheeler road below. TURN RIGHT and continue on this road.

Again this is a nice pleasant easy stroll. It crosses several small streams, then TURNS LEFT off of the road once again. It drops down to another bench, picks up another old road and stays on it for a while. This old road is not used by four–wheelers so it is easy to get on and off of. There are some nice rocks and bluffs to the right. And a little further, the trail leaves this old road TO THE LEFT, and heads down a steep hill past 23.0. Spirits Creek becomes visible from here. When you finally come off the hill and get to the creek, TURN LEFT and go upstream.

I camped at this spot once a long time ago during a winter hike with OHTA. I emphasize *winter* 'cause sometime during the night, I woke up, looked out the tent, and realized that everyone else was awake too. It took us a while to figure out what is was that woke everyone up. The creek had all of a sudden *frozen solid!* And the silence got us all up. It was about five below zero then. There are some nice camp spots in this area — just be sure that you get at least 200 feet away from the trail and the creek.

The trail heads upstream, bumps up onto a bench above the creek, then comes back down near the creek again. The trail used to cross the creek three times, but we recently rerouted it so now the trail remains on the west side longer, passing underneath a neat bluffline (tons of wildflowers here in the spring, and waterfalls, an SSS), then drops back down into the bottomland and makes the only crossing of Spirits Creek at 23.6.

During really wet periods there are lots and lots of waterfalls in this area. Some of them are very large. During the winter you'll find lots of big ice flows too. And just upstream of the creek crossing is another of my SSS's. There are a number of waterfalls on the creek, pools and slick–rock. There is also an overhang under the bluff that will keep rain off of you for a while if needed. A great area to spend some time.

The trail leaves the creek on an old road, heads uphill, levels off and then TURNS RIGHT off of the road. It continues uphill, working its way up the benches to 24.0. This is one of my SSS's. I'm not sure why, but something about this spot has always intrigued me. There is a small stream and several small hills scattered about.

From there the trail maintains its uphill pace, up a couple of benches, across a jeep road, and up to another bench where there is a nice view up and down the valley below. It crosses another jeep road, runs level for a while, and crosses a couple of four–wheeler trails. Be alert in this area and follow the white blazes.

Then the trail does one of our favorite things, it heads uphill again! But not for too long, 'cause it soon levels out and crosses FR# 1509 at 24.8. This is also known as Ragtown Road, named after a logging community that was near here many years ago.

The trail goes over the hill and down the other side where it intersects with a jeep road. TURN RIGHT and follow the road for just a little ways, then TURN RIGHT again and continue on a lesser old road. The trail is heading south, and we will eventually swing around on the north side of Black Mountain, which during leaf–off you would be able to see right now.

The trail climbs just a little and TURNS LEFT off of the road and back into the woods on trail only. It drops down just a little, then levels off and works its way around into a steep ravine. There is some nice big timber in this area. And the hill is VERY steep, although the trail remains level.

There is a class B waterfall just below the trail as it crosses a small stream that is also full of moss–covered rocks. As you look around you are looking at some of the most rugged country in the Ozarks. There are ferns, giant trees, lush mosses, and lots of waterfalls during the wet season. I've been told it's places like this where God hangs out. Of course this is one of my SSS's.

We swing to the east, and come out of the woods into an area that is now home to giant briar bushes! It's almost a tunnel effect as you hike through it. And as you come into a kind of open area, there is a four–wheeler trail that goes straight ahead, but the trail TURNS RIGHT here and continues on through the heavy brush on an old road.

Before long the trail leaves this old road and TURNS LEFT and drops down off of the hill rather steeply, past 26.0 and intersects with a motorcycle trail. TURN RIGHT here, and continue down a steep grade into and across a small creek.

This creek is an important one. If you were at this spot sixty years ago and turned around and looked out from the hill, you would have seen a huge wooden trestle spanning this ravine, and perhaps an old steam engine chugging across with a load of giant white oak trees in tow. Just downstream of the trail crossing you can look around and find several concrete pilings and large bolts and maybe other artifacts left of the trestle. There is a large class C waterfall there too. And you might even see some of the huge timbers that made up the trestle below it. PLEASE don't remove any of these artifacts. They are part of the history of the Ozarks and now of the trail. Enjoy them with eye and camera so that others may do the same.

From this creek crossing the trail climbs up onto the other end of the trestle at 26.1. It's perfectly flat, and you can look back and see how the hill was built up for the first part of the trestle. This is a neat area to hang around in a while and explore, and remember. An SSS.

This railroad bed is one of the great historical features of the OHT. It was built back in the early 1900's to help remove timber from this area. It is part of the Combs to Cass spur of the railroad that ran from Fayetteville to St. Paul. As you hike this flat corridor you can look around and see all kinds of reminders of the old railroad. There are several spots where a narrow cut takes you through the hillside. And other areas, less obvious, where the bed had to be built up quite a bit. One of the neat things to me is the fact that the tracks were taken up so long ago, that there are trees growing in the middle of the bed that are just as big as any you'll see out in the forest. As is usually the case, Mother Nature is reclaiming her land!

The trail runs on top of this railroad bed for most of the next two and a half miles. Leaving the grade only to go around another ravine that used to have another trestle in it. It's a great hike. Take your time and enjoy it. There are several roads and other trails that come onto or leave the railroad bed. Ignore all of them and stay on the level grade.

The trail goes through a couple of the narrow cuts that I mentioned, then leaves the bed and swings around another ravine that had a trestle in it. There are remains of the trestle in this ravine too. The trail rejoins the railroad on the other side.

There is another cut out area has a giant squared–off boulder sitting right in the middle of it, and 27.0 nearby. All through this area there are nice views to the north of the Fane Creek valley and the hills beyond. As a boy I "grew up" in those hills, wandering around forever toting a heavy rifle in search of deer. I was seldom successful in bagging any game, but I sure learned a lot about the outdoors, and about myself.

After you pass through the fourth cut out area, you may see a spot where the bed had to be built up a great deal. It must have taken a lot of work to put this railroad together. And their work will last many lifetimes. This section contains the longest, straightest and most level piece of the OHT that I know of. Trail continues past on 28.0.

You may see an ancient barbwire corral on the left that was probably used to keep in some sort of livestock. And there are some bluffs and small overhangs in the area, and a fifth cut out area. Not too far beyond this last area, the trail TURNS LEFT and leaves the railroad bed, then drops down into the woods past 29.0.

The trail winds its way down through the forest, losing some elevation, but not too much. It eventually comes alongside a wildlife food plot. It skirts around the plot, crosses an old road, and passes a wildlife pond.

The trail makes a sharp left and begins a pretty good drop down off of the hill past 30.0. It swings back around to the right, and levels out on the bottom next to Fane Creek. It follows the creek for a while, then turns left and crosses Fane Creek at 30.3. Unless you want to spend a lot of time looking around for a better crossing, you will normally have to cross here wet. The creek flows across a flat rock, and most of the creek piles up on the near side, making it impossible to cross dry.

At normal water levels, the other side of the flat rock usually sticks out and leaves plenty of room to lay around and rest awhile. You may need the rest, 'cause from this point, you've got about a 1500–foot climb up to and across Whiting Mountain.

Something else that you should think about is water. Fane Creek is really the last year–round water source on the trail until Herrods Creek, which is nearly 16 miles away at 46.2. During most of the year there are probably dozens and dozens of small creeks that you will cross, so you don't have to worry too much about it. But if a lot of the small creeks that you have been crossing have been dry, then you should stock up now and be safe.

From the creek the trail snakes its way up to the first bench where it crosses FR# 1520 (Fane Cr. Road). If you turned right and followed this road it would take you to the community of Cass about a mile away. (Turner Bend is another 1.5 miles down Hwy. 23) The trail crosses the road at an angle — it continues in the woods about 50 feet to the right.

It begins the uphill climb right away, and works its way up a bench or two, then levels off, then up again, crossing a couple of jeep roads, four–wheeler trails, and a small creek. It eventually climbs up onto the nose of a ridge where it intersects with a jeep road. TURN LEFT on this road. Bear to the right soon after, and then the road sort of disappears and the trail becomes just trail again.

The trail crosses through an eroding ditch, then swings to the left and goes uphill. It continues up the hill, with a turn here and there, and a few places of level grade. There are some trees off to the right that are blazed with red paint. This is private property, and the trail swings up and around this area to miss it.

After the second batch of red blazes, past which the trail goes up and around, it levels out a bit. The trail then makes its way through several small creeks, then heads uphill at a pretty steep grade.

The trail turns to the left, climbs up some more, then swings around through some large boulders and comes out into a "regeneration area." This is basically a part of the forest that they have deadened all of the trees in, then left them to die. The idea was to plant pines to replace the hardwoods.

The trail goes right through the middle of this area, which used to be quite miserable to hike through. This was the main reason why we now have a protected corridor so that this sort of thing does not happen again. Once the overstory trees are removed, the brush that grows up afterwards is terrible, and remains so for years. The area gets pretty grown up in the summer, and shorts are *not* recommended here!

The trail does go into a nice wooded area that wasn't cut, then turns uphill and snakes its way through a bunch of sharp rocks. It eventually turns back to the right, climbs up some more, then runs fairly level. You are on the upper end of the regeneration area, and at one time there where were some pretty nice views looking down into the Mulberry River Valley and the community of Cass.

The trail runs just below a real nice rock wall, then uphill a little at first. Then it gets serious and switchbacks up the hill at a steady pace.

It eventually comes out on top of Whiting Mountain, and crosses a natural gas pipeline near 34.0. From here the trail drops down the other side of the hill, and begins its descent down to Hwy. 23. It passes large boulders, then levels off through some nice forest.

Still fairly level, the trail goes alongside a short bluff, with a couple of small overhangs. Just downhill from the trail is Hwy. 23. You may be able to see it here and there, and certainly hear cars on it. The trail eventually drops down the hill, then level past 35.0, and then passes a spur trail at 35.2 that goes up the hill to the left just a short ways to the rockhouse shelter, another SSS.

This shelter was built back near the turn of the century and was used by different families of loggers as a home over the years. It has a cement floor, and way in the back, there is a spring, kind of. The walls are beginning to separate from the ceiling, but it will still turn away the rain.

From the rockhouse spur intersection the main trail heads downhill and eventually levels off on a bench and comes to another intersection and trail register at 35.4. TURN RIGHT and follow the blue-blazed spur trail and you will come out on Hwy. 23 at the Cherry Bend Trailhead parking area, ending this section at 35.5. GPS 35.74337° N, -93.81152° W

If you are hiking past Cherry Bend, the main trail continues straight ahead past the registration box, drops down to and across a wooden foot bridge that was built by boy scouts, and then crosses Hwy. 23 at 35.5.

SECTION THREE — 19.8 miles
Cherry Bend Trailhead/Hwy. 23 to Lick Branch Trailhead

Trail Point	Mile Point	Mileage West–East	Mileage East-West
Cherry Bend TH/Hwy. 23	35.4 + .1 spur	0.0	19.8
E. Fly Gap Rd./FR# 1503	39.1	3.8	16.0
Hare Mountain	41.3	6.0	13.8
FR# 1504	43.0	7.7	12.1
Hare Mountain/ Morgan Fields Trailhead	43.1	7.8	12.0
Redding/Spy Rock Spur	45.1	9.8	10.0
Herrods Creek	46.2	10.9	8.9
Williams Falls	47.0	11.7	8.1
Cobb Ridge	48.1	13.8	6.0
Indian Creek	50.0	14.7	5.1
Spur to Indian Creek TH	50.9	15.6	4.2
Indian Creek TH/Hwy. 215	50.9 + .7 spur	16.3	4.9
Briar Branch (Marinoni Scenic Area)	52.5	17.2	2.6
Lick Branch Trailhead FR# 1497/CR# 5051	55.1	19.8	0.0

This section begins at the Cherry Bend Trailhead on Hwy. 23 (a National Scenic Byway). It is located about midway between the community of Cass and Brashears. This section is located on the Pleasant Hill Ranger District (office in Clarksville). Quad maps are Cass and Yale. GPS 35.74337° N, -93.81152° W

This 19.8 miles of trail is one of the more scenic sections of the trail. It goes up to and over historic Hare Mountain, the highest point on the OHT. It passes many nice waterfalls. Then makes its way through the Indian Creek area, which is one of the most remote spots on the Forest. It passes through the Marinoni Scenic Area, a small canyon with high bluffs and huge beech trees. And ends at the Lick Branch Trailhead Parking Area. If you are hiking in the dry season, you probably won't see any water 'til Herrods Creek at 46.5, so you should be sure and carry plenty.

*Note a major landslide in 2021 will require a reroute in the 37-38mm area so trail route may be different than described.

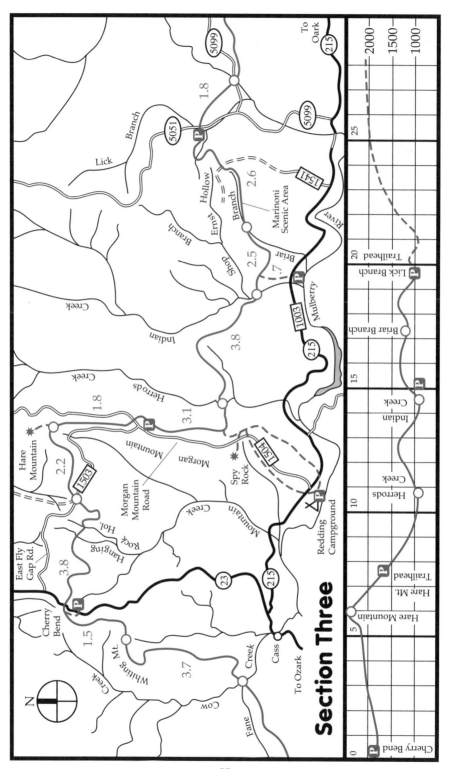

Section Three

The trail begins across the highway from the parking lot on Hwy. 23. It goes up into the woods on a blue-blazed spur trail that intersects with the main trail coming from White Rock Mountain. Turn left at the registration box to head back towards White Rock, Shores Lake and Lake Ft. Smith. TURN RIGHT at the box and you will continue east on the trail. It drops down to and across a wooden footbridge built by boy scouts, then crosses Hwy. 23 in the middle of a sharp curve (this is where the name "Cherry Bend" comes from). *Stop* and listen for oncoming traffic before you cross here.

It continues into the woods past 36.0 and runs along a jeep road for a short while, then TURNS RIGHT off of the road. It drops down a couple of benches, crosses a couple of small streams, then works its way back up a couple of benches. Just before it intersects an old jeep road, the trail TURNS RIGHT, crosses a small stream, then goes along the edge of a mostly-level bench.

Roy Senyard Falls is located below the trail in the 36.0+ area via a quarter mile+ difficult bushwhack (no trail, steep terrain, unmarked — GPS 35.74328, -93.80773). Roy was the maintenance coordinator of this trail for more than two decades, and was the heart and soul of the OHT. During the wet season it is a beautiful waterfall and cascade, and Murray Falls is right next door. See my **Arkansas Waterfalls** *guidebook.*

The trail crosses the old jeep road, heads up into the woods past an old homesite, then intersects with another road trace— TURN LEFT. It runs pretty much level, and passes through forest that is full of large hardwoods and thick underbrush.

The trail drops off the hill a little, crosses a couple of small creeks, eases back up the hill, up and around a small nose of a ridge, and passes some nice rock formations. It turns to the north, then back to the east along some long, straight, level stretches of trail. There are some nice views in this area. One of the things that you can see to the south is Mulberry Mountain, a lodge and event center that is next to Hwy. 23.

The trail joins an old roadbed, heads uphill, and then TURNS LEFT off of the roadbed. Just at the top of this small hill the trail intersects with a jeep road. TURN LEFT here, continue on the road for only a hundred feet or so, then TURN LEFT off of the road and continue straight into the woods, past a kind of mini rock quarry.

It works its way up along the top of a ridge, swings to the right, then drops down to and crosses FR# 1503 at 39.1. This road is also East Fly Gap Road, and this area is known as Fly Gap. The trail goes across this road and skirts around a makeshift parking area that is off to the right. It continues into the woods off to the left of this area. There is an old roadbed that takes off from the back of the parking area so be sure that you are on the trail.

From the road the trail eases its way up the hill just a little, then levels off. When the hillside gets real steep around you, during leaf–off you can look up the hill and see a nice rock wall that was built up on top of the hill. Although I've never gone up and explored, there is probably an old homesite up there. Like Hare Mountain coming up, many of the flat–topped hills in the Ozarks were once farmed, and many of these walls were built around the edges. You will get a close up view of one of the best examples of these walls on Hare Mountain.

The trail continues around the north side of this hill, and gets back to more level surroundings. It follows an apparent old roadbed a bit , then leaves this roadbed to the RIGHT. From here the land gets steep again, then the trail turns back to the south, joins another old roadbed, and everything around you levels off. The trail through all of this remains fairly level. In this area if you can see off to the east, the large hill that you are looking at is Hare Mountain.

The trail leaves the old roadbed and drops down to and across a small stream. Although tiny in size, I have often filled my empty water bottles from this little wonder. It is usually dry in August and September for sure, like most everything else.

From this stream the trail works its way around another hill, where you can get a better look at Hare Mountain as you get closer. It's not a towering mountain like you might expect, but rather a flat–topped one that is nestled in with several others, so it doesn't look real impressive.

The trail goes through a saddle between the two hills, then begins a climb of a couple hundred feet up to Hare Mountain. It swings back and forth at a constant, but not too steep grade, passing 41.0. When you top out and are walking on a sort of rock shelf, then you have made it, and are at the highest point on the OHT at about 2380 feet.

The trail is level here, and is actually running just above a small bluff. Out to the right there is a wonderful view to the south down into the Mulberry River Valley. You can also look out and see a ridge extending to the south from Hare Mountain — this is where the trail will go next. And just uphill from the trail you will find one of the best examples of a pioneer rock wall in the Ozarks.

This wall was built by an early settler who cleared this mountaintop and grew corn, cotton, and whatever else he needed to live on. The trail follows the wall for about 800 feet, then swings to the right and heads down the ridge that I just spoke of. As the trail turns there is a great view of the surrounding countryside at 41.8. And if you look almost due south from here, off in the distance about as far as you can see, you may spot Mt. Magazine, which is the highest point in Arkansas at 2753 feet. It is actually on the other side of the Arkansas River. The view is terrific, but unfortunately the view to the west is blocked by a hill, so there isn't much of a view of the sunset.

There is a spur trail here that heads back to the left/north (blue blazes), and leads to a primitive campsite. There is a large rock firepit there that has been built up over the years by OHTA members. We have a hike–in here each October to celebrate our anniversary. There is plenty of level space to camp even the largest army of hikers. And from the firepit, if you head to the right there is a small trail that leads back to the old homesite. There is a nice rock chimney there, and a hand–dug well. There is usually water in the well (under the rock lid), but I would filter it before use. It is about 15 feet deep, and sometimes almost dries up — so don't count on it during the dry season!

There is another water source nearby during much of the year. From the firepit, head north-ish into the woods. You will see a low spot on the hill. Head down into this low spot. It gets real steep, but if you follow it down, you will eventually come to a small creek that forms. It's a tough climb out, but if you are stuck on the mountain and need water, it's a cheap price to pay. Once again, don't count on this water during the dry season. And if you are camping on the mountain, use the primitive campsite — *please* don't camp back at the viewpoint. There is a glade area there that looks inviting but won't take much traffic.

Needless to say, Hare Mountain is one of my most favorite

SSS's! You will enjoy it too, so plan to stay a while, inspect the historical sites and enjoy the view. Be extra careful though — there is often a lot of bear activity in the area. In fact, this is the site of the first recorded "attack" of a human by a bear in Arkansas. David Gasche from Wichita, Kansas was bitten once by a large bear (May 23rd, 1990) while still in his tent. He got a nasty wound, but did manage to eventually escape. The only real thing that he did wrong was to not scream at the bear when he first saw it rummaging through his pack (his food was hung, but the bear got it).

I talked with David the day that he was bitten, and he told me a pretty scary story. I won't go through the whole thing here. But I will tell you one tidbit. After the bear bit him, David stayed in his sleeping bag inside his tent while the bear nosed around for nearly an hour. At one point, the bear grabbed his tent (with David inside!) and drug the whole mess off into the woods. Good grief! I think I would lose it right then and there. (After David left the area, the bear came back and drug off his sleeping bag — I found it a couple of hundred yards away the next day.)

We have installed a bear pole* to hang your food on at the firepit — be sure that you camp away from this immediate area, just in case someone gets hungry! By the way, most bear encounters are in the early morning. Back to the trail.

From the viewpoint, the trail heads south, down the top of a genuine "razorback." The ridge is very narrow here. You can get a good view of the sunrise, and will be looking down into the Herrods Creek drainage. There is a deer hunter's cabin visible, but besides that what you are looking at is one of the most remote sections of the Ozark National Forest. And you can see many ridges beyond. The trail will eventually go up and over most of them.

From here the trail drops off, remaining on the ridge, and passes a nice view that looks off to the south and west. You get a good look at Mulberry Mountain from here.

The trail continues down the top of the ridge, crossing an old road, then swings around to the left side of the ridge, missing a wildlife food plot. It rises just a little, then swings to the right side of the ridge and passes another nice short wall.

It skirts around a clearcut area that was an early battleground between OHTA and the Forest Service concerning the trail corridor. There was a beautiful stand of giant pine trees here. It was a nice, peaceful walk. We lost and most of the big trees were cut down, but were able to get them to save a few nice big pines along the trail. This will never happen again since we finally won out and now have a protected trail corridor.

From here the trail runs over to the left side of the ridge and works its way down, passing through a young stand of pines, then to and across FR# 1504 at 43.0. The trail from Hare Mountain to this point was the first section of trail that was built by OHTA way back in the winter of 1981.

The trail drops below the road and turns to the right. Just after it crosses a couple of small streams, there is a trail intersection at 43.1. Turn right and a short spur (blue blazes) takes you up to the Hare Mountain/Morgan Fields Trailhead parking lot. The main trail continues STRAIGHT AHEAD.

It winds around, crosses a jeep road, a small creek, then works around just below a field, and drops down onto a rocky bench. If you can see out through the trees, look across to the opposite hillside and a little south. There is a low spot in the ridge (Cobb Ridge). The trail passes through that saddle at 48.1.

The trail works its way into a small ravine (an SSS), crossing the creek there, then continues out across the same bench. After a nice level hike, the trail drops over the edge of the bench. It passes under a huge oak tree, and crosses a small rocky creek. Right next to the trail on this creek is a class B waterfall known as Waterfall #1 at 44.8. There are four of these falls between here and Herrods Creek (#1, #2, #3 & #4).

The trail drops down and across a couple more benches. Directly across the valley from here is the saddle that I spoke of earlier. Into another little ravine the trail goes, and crosses two small creeks. Just below the trail the second one pours off of Waterfall #2, a class C falls. This little area is another one of my SSS's, and is worth some time to look around.

Past Waterfall #2 the trail works its way around the hill and down through several broken benches. It rises up just a little and crosses a jeep road. It continues on the level through a rock field, then comes to a trail intersection at 45.1. The trail to the right (blue blazes) goes about a mile to Spy Rock lookout, and connects to a loop trail that comes out of Redding Campground. There is a separate map and description of this loop trail on page 151.

(If you are heading to Redding or Spy Rock from this direction, here is a brief description. The spur runs along fairly level for about a half mile, then forks. The right fork goes across FR# 1504, then on out to the end of a ridge to a point known as Spy Rock. There is a good view up and down the valley in front, as well as down into the Mulberry River Valley. There are some nice, broken bluffs here too.

If you turn left at the fork, the trail continues down towards Redding Campground. In a little while there is another intersection. The right turn becomes the West Loop, the left turn the East Loop. The West Loop is a little bit shorter. They both meet at the bottom near the river and lead into Redding Campground (when the West Loop meets the East Loop, turn right to get to the campground). It's about 4.4 miles from the main trail to the campground using the West Loop, which by the way I would recommend you take since it is in much better shape.)

Now back up on the main trail at the Redding Spur intersection, the trail GOES STRAIGHT here and continues to work its way down the hill. It swings around down through the benches and comes to a spur trail (blue blazes) that goes off to the right. This short (200 feet) spur leads to Waterfall #3, a class B falls.

From here the trail comes alongside a neat little stream, and follows it downhill. Waterfalls #3 & #4 are both on this stream. It is a rocky area, and when wet is one of my SSS's. The trail leaves the stream, swings to the left and drops over the hill, then swings back to the right. It makes a sharp turn back to the left just as it rejoins the stream. At this curve there is another spur trail (blue blazes) that heads upstream a couple hundred feet to Waterfall #4, a class C falls, and another SSS.

The water here flows over moss–covered ledges and makes a really pretty scene. It is pictured in the *National Geographic* book "America's Hidden Corners" on page 159. (This was my first *National Geographic* picture!)

The main trail continues downstream alongside this neat little stream, and then crosses it. Just beyond it swings back to the left and crosses Herrods Creek at 46.2. It actually crosses in two sections, and can be crossed most of the time dry. During the spring you'll have to wade.

As it crosses the creek there is a jeep road off to the left. Be sure and stay on the trail as it goes to the RIGHT into a cedar thicket. As the trail comes out of the cedars, it crosses a jeep road, then swings to the left and into the woods. If you need to get off the trail in an emergency, take this road to the right and you will come out (across private property) Hwy. 215 that runs along the Mulberry River (about a mile from the trail).

The trail swings around a hill, then crosses a stream. It then begins to work its way up the hill, coming next to another small stream, then veers back to and overlooks the stream that we just crossed. Just across the stream there is a nice bluffline visible. The view down into the stream is nice, and there are some large boulders along the trail as well.

From here it continues the gradual climb up the hill, and eventually winds around past mile 47.0 and to a small overlook of Williams Falls, a class C waterfall. This falls and just upstream is another of my SSS's. The falls were named after OHTA member John Strait Williams, who was the first person that I ever saw swim here in the winter!

The trail turns to the left, still following the stream as it continues to climb. Then it swings sharply back to the left, then the right, and gets a little more serious about going up. It eventually levels off a bit, and crosses a small creek.

From here the trail passes through a thick area where the trees were killed, left in place to rot, and pine trees planted. It passes below a pond, then rises up past 48.0 to the top of the hill at 48.1 named Cobb Ridge.

It crosses a jeep road on top (Beech Grove Road), then drops down the hill and turns back to the right. It works its way down into and across a small drainage. There is a large tree here that you might admire, and a nice waterfall just above where the trail crosses. This is pretty typical of the way that the trail runs from here down to Indian Creek, which, by the way, is the drainage that you are in now. The trail crosses several of these small creeks, all with nice waterfalls both above and below the trail.

Beyond this first creek, the trail continues to drop gradually, and passes 49.0. It also begins to pass large beech trees. They are the ones with the smooth bark that all the idiots of the world like to carve their initials in. This does nothing except advertise to the world just how stupid they really are! You will see a lot of these wonderful beech trees along the trail for a while, hopefully they will remain unmarked. By the way, beech trees (especially young ones) keep their leaves during the winter. It's nice to hear their golden leaves rustling in the breeze on a crisp January day.

The trail crosses another creek past more large timber, and a class C waterfall below the trail. In fact there is an overhang down there that you might seek refuge under during a rainstorm. And all along this area during leaf–off you will have lots of nice views up and down the Indian Creek drainage. This area, as I have mentioned before, is one of the most rugged and remote areas in the state. It was proposed as a wilderness area in the early 80's, but lost out to timber interests.

The trail crosses another creek or two with more waterfalls, then drops downhill. It crosses an old jeep road, comes along Indian Creek for just a couple of hundred feet, then comes out on another jeep road. TURN LEFT here and cross Indian Creek at 50.0. This is almost always a wet crossing. The jeep road also crosses here (if you take this road back to the right you will come out, across private property, on Hwy. 215 that runs along the Mulberry River).

On the other side, stay TO THE RIGHT of the jeep road and head into the woods. After a short level stretch, the trail begins its climb out of the Indian Creek drainage. It works its way to the right up the hill, crossing a couple of small creeks. There are a few level spots, but mainly it's a steady climb. The view on the way up is great, especially during leaf–off. Across the way you can see a field and a couple of cabins. And off to the south, the fields that lie along the Mulberry River are visible.

The trail continues uphill, and enters another regeneration area. It swings around the end of the hill, levels off and crosses a jeep road and a trail intersection at 50.9. The spur trail to the right (downhill) goes .7 miles down to the Indian Creek Trailhead and Canoe Launch on the Mulberry River just across Hwy. 215 (don't leave your car here long-term if there is a chance of flooding). This spur trail was built in honor of our great friend and longtime trail advocate and volunteer, Dawna Robinson. We miss her...

The main trail goes STRAIGHT AHEAD across the jeep road, then a small creek, past 51.0, and leaves the regeneration area. It eases up the hill a little, then levels off. It eventually enters a nice stand of large pines, and runs along the edge of a steep dropoff. You are heading up into the Briar Branch drainage, and can look up into it, and into the Marinoni Scenic Area.

As the trail begins to drop off of the hill if you are quiet you can hear the rush of Briar Branch Falls. This is a class C falls and is on the creek a ways down the hill below the trail.

The trail continues to drop down the hill gradually, and eventually rises up just a tad and hits an old jeep road. TURN RIGHT on this road, and follow it just a short distance downhill to Briar Branch. At this point, just before you cross the creek, there is a nice camping spot off to the right. And just across the creek up on the hillside, there are some windblown formations in the sandstone bluff there. Also, downstream about a quarter of a mile is the waterfall that I mentioned earlier.

Straight ahead the trail crosses Briar Branch at 52.5, and enters the Marinoni Scenic Area, a major SSS of mine. This little area is one of the highlights of the OHT. It was named after Paul A. Marinoni, a longtime resident of Fayetteville, and a good friend of mine. As I was growing up he taught me a great deal about the outdoors, the value of them, and how we need to preserve them for all generations to enjoy and learn from. He and my dad, another great outdoorsman, were best of friends. There is a wonderful little canyon just north of here that is named after my dad.

Once across the creek the trail climbs up a bench or two, crosses a small stream, then eases up just a little more. It crosses another stream in between two class B–C waterfalls, one just above the trail, the other just below. From here you enter the heart of the Scenic Area. There is a bluff on the right that grows next to the trail. The beech trees get bigger, and there is a nice view below of Briar Branch, tumbling over moss–covered rocks.

At one point the trail comes right up next to this towering bluff. This is simply a great place to come and wander around and enjoy all the beauty that we have here. The bluff in this area has a lot of ferns and other vegetation growing on it. And there are a lot of umbrella magnolia trees growing here too. In the springtime they are in full bloom, with giant blossoms!

The trail passes a small overhang, the end of the bluff, and crosses a small creek. A couple of hundred feet beyond this creek there is another bluff that begins up to the right. At this spot there is a natural rock bridge that arches across the top of the bluff. It's a small bridge, but well worth the short climb up to it. Also, just above the bridge, there is a large bunch of wild azalea bushes that come into bloom during May. If you have just walked through this wonderful little area for the first time, you'll understand just what I mean by an "SSS"!

From here the trail crosses Briar Branch again, heads up into a tiny canyon for a few feet, then swings back over Briar Branch. It comes down to and crosses the creek a total of three more times. After the last crossing, way up in the headwaters, the trail swings uphill and crosses a jeep road on top at 53.2 (Briar Ridge Road). If you need to get out you can turn right on this road, and it will eventually turn into FR# 1541, which comes out onto Hwy. 215 after several miles.

Once across the jeep road the trail turns to the left and begins to drop down the hill. There is a great view from here of the Little Mulberry River Valley and the hills beyond. The trail runs across a level, rocky bench for a while, then swings around the nose of a small ridge. It continues on the level, and begins to run just above a small bluff line.

At one point, the bluff actually becomes the trail tread, and it runs along the top of it. Then the trail makes a SHARP TURN TO THE RIGHT and descends down through this bluff. This spot is another one of my SSS's. A nice spot to lay around for a while.

As it goes through the bluff the trail swings back to the left, then turns and heads downhill a little out into the woods. It continues gradually downhill, swings right, then left, cutting back into the hillside. It lands on a narrow bench and levels off.

This is a rocky bench, and just over the edge it is pretty steep country. The bench disappears as the trail heads down the slope. It turns into the hillside and crosses a small creek, and continues down the hill past a couple of nice, large boulders. As it comes around the hill a powerline right of way comes into view. At this point you are looking down across a creek right at the Lick Branch Trailhead.

The trail drops off the hill and crosses the creek (sometimes a wet crossing, sometimes dry), then turns right and heads downstream. The trailhead is to the left, or straight ahead the trail comes out to and across FR# 1497/CR# 5051 at 55.1, and the end of this section. GPS 35.71000° N, -93.66157° W

SECTION FOUR — 29.6 miles
Lick Branch Trailhead to Ozone Campground TH (Hwy. 21)

Trail Point	Mile Point	Mileage West–East	Mileage East–West
Lick Branch Trailhead **FR# 1497/CR# 5051**	55.1	0.0	29.6
Little Mulberry Cr. Bridge	56.9	1.8	27.8
Little Mulberry Overlook	60.5	5.4	24.2
FR# 1453/CR# 6200	64.7	9.6	20.0
Lynn Hollow Creek	69.1	14.0	15.6
Arbaugh Road Trailhead **FR# 1404/CR# 5261**	70.0	14.9	14.7
Lewis Prong Cr. first cross	72.0	16.9	12.7
Lewis Prong Cr. last cross	74.5	19.3	10.3
Waterfall Hollow Creek	77.0	21.9	7.7
Moonhull Mountain	77.5	22.4	7.2
Boomer Branch	81.0	25.9	3.7
Mulberry River	83.3	28.2	1.4
FR# 1003/CR# 5440	83.4	28.3	1.3
Ozone CG TH (Hwy. 21)	84.7	29.6	0.0

This 29.6 mile section is the longest, and one of the least used. There are long stretches with not much scenery, but there are also a lot of interesting things to see. This is a good section to hike when you think the other sections might be too crowded (which as of yet has not happened — the OHT is still one of the best–kept secrets in the hiking community). It is all located on the Pleasant Hill Ranger District. Quad maps are Yale, Oark, Boston, Fallsville and Ozone. GPS 35.71000° N, -93.66157° W

The trail crosses both the Mulberry and Little Mulberry Rivers, has some spectacular views into both valleys, and passes by a number of waterfalls. There are some pretty steep climbs, and there is a lot of walking on old roads.

This section begins at the Lick Branch Trailhead, mile #55.1. You can reach the trailhead from Hwy. 215 (the Mulberry River Road), by turning north on CR# 5099 at Yale, then left on CR# 5051 (also FR# 1497, watch for the sign). The parking lot is to the left, just after you cross a small creek on a short bridge.

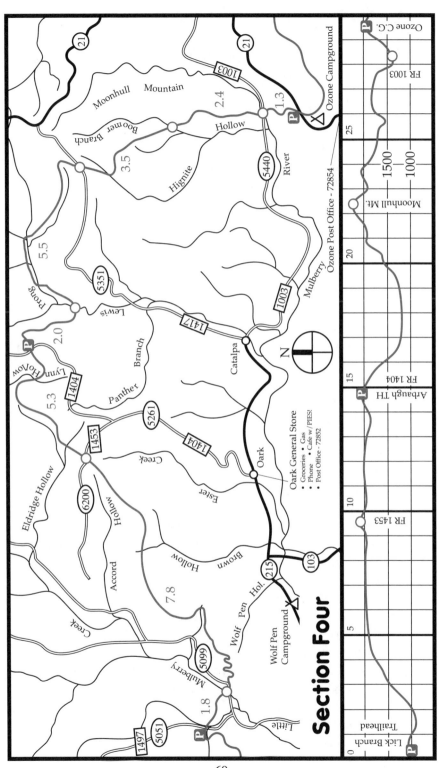

Section Four

Oark General Store
• Groceries • Gas
• Phone • Cafe w/ PIES!
• Post Office - 72852

Ozone Post Office - 72854

From the parking lot, the trail crosses FR# 1497/CR# 5051, and then Lick Branch. The trail continues on the other side, turning to the right (downstream). In a short distance it heads up the hillside, climbing up to the first bench. It's kind of rocky for a while.

Shortly, the trail climbs up onto the next bench, where it will stay for a little while. Here the trail passes through one of my SSS's — an area with several house–sized boulders and huge beech trees. This is a good spot to linger for a while if you have the time. The bench continues to be level, and *very* rocky.

Eventually, the trail makes a sharp turn to the left, then switchbacks uphill, past a couple of large beech trees, onto another, less rocky bench.

The trail continues on this bench for a while, then makes its way to the left, up the hill. It climbs some more, up and around the south side of the hill. There are some good views down into the usually lush fields of the Little Mulberry River Valley. It levels off for a while, then begins to descend gradually, crossing a couple of old roads.

Looking to the east, you can see a large mountain looming before you. If you are continuing on past Little Mulberry, this will be your next climb, and is one of the largest on the trail. Enjoy the view while you can!

On the way down, the trail goes into a narrow band of cedar trees, then across a small slough–type creek. It looks like it is one long slab of rock, going downhill, covered with moss and other slippery green stuff.

Beyond the slough, the trail continues downhill through more rocky terrain, then levels off a bit. It crosses an old road, drops down further, and crosses a small creek. Just beyond this point you may notice a bunch of red paint to the left. This marks a private property corner. From here the trail runs to the south, down alongside a small creek in a narrow band of timber that is wedged in between two pastures. This is the only section of the trail corridor where an easement had to be purchased.

This odd little section ends up on the county road where the trail TURNS LEFT, and follows the road to a bridge over the Little Mulberry Creek at 56.95. Cross over the bridge, and about 50 feet beyond TURN RIGHT off the road.

A set of steps leads down off the road, then the trail starts up the hillside into the woods. It turns right, and begins a long, 1,000 foot switchback climb up, past mile 57.0. There is lots to see along the way — like large boulders and some really nice big timber. It climbs a while, levels off a bit, then more uphill. 58.0 is about two thirds of the way up.

From this spot, the trail climbs up some more, then turns to the north and levels off for the most part, crossing several small streams. During leaf–off you can begin to get some nice views, looking up and down the Little Mulberry valley. And the climbing is basically finished.

The trail comes around the edge of a deep little ravine, and crosses a small creek (some water most of the year). This area would make a neat little camp spot. There is plenty of level ground, water, and the bluffs and waterfalls in this little ravine just downstream make for great exploring. This is another one of my SSS's.

From here the trail continues past 59.0 on the level, kind of wandering around through the woods. It eventually works its way uphill a little, then soon levels off, and this is the sign that the climbing is finished! There is a rock wall that you may see here that is kind of the boundary of the mountaintop fields in this area, and the trail stays on this edge of the mountaintop for a while. At about 60.5 it runs on top of the bluffline to one of the best views on the entire trail, the Little Mulberry Overlook.

The trail leaves the edge of the hillside, goes through a pine plantation (planted in the early 1980's), and turns back to the right, crossing this flat–topped ridge. It skirts around the plantation, crosses a jeep road, passes by a wildlife pond, turns left and runs pretty much on the level through the woods and across another road.

The trail curves around to the right a little, crosses a small stream just below another wildlife pond. There is another property boundary marker — lots of red paint. From here the trail bends around to the left and makes its way across the flat ridgetop once again. It crosses a jeep road, goes through a stand of pines, crosses a couple more jeep roads, then back into hardwoods again.

The trail bends around to the right, staying fairly level. In this area you are looking down into Accord Hollow, a deep drainage to the north that is home to several waterfalls, including the

61' tall Accord Hollow Falls (detailed in my *Arkansas Waterfalls* guidebook).

The trail swings around the upper reaches of Accord Hollow, then turns to the right, crosses a road, then curves around a ridge. It begins to climb a little, turning to the left, and looks down on a jeep road. It follows just above this road for a little while, climbing a little more, crosses this jeep road, and then continues into the woods on the level.

It bumps up onto a bench of small pine trees, then back into open hardwoods. It runs level for a while, then climbs up a couple of benches, up to and across FR# 1453/CR# 6200 at 64.7. This is the closest that you will get to the community of Oark. It is about five miles down this forest road to the right. There is a general store and post office there (*terrific* cafe too!!!).

From the road, the trail begins to drop downhill. Just after the second switchback, there is an interesting rock buried right in the trail. I have seen this strange type of formation called many different things, but I'll just call it a weird rock and let you come to your own conclusion.

The trail continues downhill through a thick hardwood forest. It crosses a couple of small streams and levels off. It winds its way around, and crosses several more streams. This begins what I call the Eldridge Hollow Waterfall Area, all of which I consider an SSS. There are a few class B falls here, then a little ways beyond, another stream with a little bigger waterfall. Just beyond this falls, you will notice a rock pit with some old rusty barrels in it up in the woods to the right. An old BBQ pit or something.

At this point, the trail begins to skirt around a regeneration area, which you can see also off to the right. The trail remains level, and follows on around the edge of a flat area. All along here you will have good views down into Eldridge Hollow. The trail continues on around the regeneration area, then drops off into a little ravine.

After the first two switchbacks down, the trail runs along on top of a bluff, and you can look down into the creek below. A couple of more switchbacks brings you down to and across this small creek. There are lots of nice rocks, bluffs and waterfalls in this spot. Another SSS. Just upstream there is a class C waterfall, and underneath it someone has built up a little rock fort. Along the same bluff, there is an overhang with plenty of room to get under during heavy rain. Spend some time in this area exploring around if you can.

The trail continues on up and out of this area, and across another small drainage, with a class B waterfall. This is all still in the Eldridge Hollow Waterfall Area. There are some nice big car-sized boulders here, and the trail winds its way through a couple of them. Then around to and across yet another stream. This one has two class C waterfalls, sort of double-decker style.

Continuing still on a level grade, the trail winds through the rock-strewn forest, then leaves the waterfall area. From here the trail climbs up and out of Eldridge Hollow, to a semi-open, partly grown up field on top. TURN RIGHT at the edge of the field, and follow it around for a couple hundred feet. Then cross the field (it's pretty narrow here) and enter the corridor in the woods. This should be well marked.

As soon as you enter the woods, you will cross a forest road, then back into the woods, and under a power line. The trail remains level for a while, then goes up just a tad and enters a thick, pine area. It crosses another forest road, then continues on the level through the pine plantation and 68.0.

The trail makes its way through the pines for a short distance, then turns left and heads slightly downhill, back into the hardwoods once again. As the trail continues on a fairly level grade, there are some good views down into Lynn Hollow. It eventually drops down a couple of steep benches, then levels off again. There is a lot of big timber in this area.

The trail runs along on top of a bluffline for a while, and you can look down into the creek bottom. You can also look up and see the opposite hillside — that is of course where the trail will go next — up and over! You cross Lynn Hollow Creek, another of my SSS's. The creek is pretty here, but a trip downstream will reveal lots more neat stuff. Bluffs, overhangs, waterfalls. A nice little area.

From the creek crossing, the trail goes to the left, up and over a small hill, then crosses a small creek. Just beyond, there is an old spur trail that goes to the left (blue blazes). It will take you back down into some of the scenic parts of Lynn Hollow. The main trail continues to the RIGHT, and climbs up the hill. It levels out on the first bench, and follows it for a while. From this bench you can look back and see the hillside that you just came off of.

The trail climbs up another two benches, and crosses a small creek. In this crossing is a stepping stone that, if you stretch your imagination, looks like the state of Arkansas. There is also a class B waterfall here. The trail continues on, and works its way around and alongside another drainage. The trail doesn't cross this creek, but does pop up over the edge of it, and passes above Lichen Falls that you can hear when it's roaring below, at about 69.8 (very steep climb down to it and dangerous!).

Then the trail comes out onto a flat area, and follows what is left of the stream out to Arbaugh Road/FR# 1404/CR# 5261 at 69.95. Across the road is the Arbaugh Road Trailhead.

The community of Oark is about seven miles to the right. Highway 16 is about three miles to the left. And in case of emergency, there is a farm down the road to the left about a half a mile.

There is a trail register here so be sure to sign in. The trail continues from the back of this trailhead, and goes out into the open woods, past a pond, and then into thick brush. The last time that I hiked this section it was in the late summer, and the ground was covered with wild plums. Small, but mighty tasty!

The trail leaves the thick area, and heads downhill, into hardwoods once again. It drops down the hillside, and lands on an old log road. TURN RIGHT on this road, and continue at a level grade. The trail leaves the old road, continues through the woods fairly level, then intersects another old road. TURN LEFT at this second road. Stay on this road all the way to the bottom. It does head on down the hill, but not too steep. On the way down you get some nice views of the Lewis Prong Creek Valley that you are dropping into.

Still on the old road, the trail crosses Lewis Prong Creek near 72.0. As you pull out of the stream bed, the trail leaves the road after about twenty feet and TURNS LEFT. This is actually just a shortcut between two roads. Then it intersects the other jeep road. TURN LEFT on this jeep road.

The trail stays on this road for almost three miles. It follows the creek upstream, gradually climbing, leveling off, then dropping down into the bottom again. While up on the hillside, there are some good views during leaf–off periods.

Not too far beyond this the trail comes alongside the creek again, then crosses it at 73.2. It continues on the road and into the woods, away from the creek. There is a lesser road that enters from the left a few hundred yards beyond — STAY on the STRAIGHT and level road. Just beyond this intersection, there is an old "root cellar" off to the right. And if you are interested in this type of stuff, you can probably kick around some and find the old home site in the area too.

The trail continues on the road, running pretty level. It crosses one creek, then not too far beyond it crosses Turner Hollow Creek, which has a solid rock slab bottom. And then the trail crosses Lewis Prong Creek at 74.5 for the last time. There is another questionable intersection a ways beyond — again take the straight and level road — it should be well marked.

Just when this road walking has about put you to sleep, and the trail has come alongside Waterfall Hollow Creek, the trail leaves the road to the LEFT. It goes up into the woods then runs pretty level, but goes through some rocky areas. It dips down into a small drainage, then comes alongside Waterfall Hollow Creek again.

The trail climbs up alongside a huge rock, then makes its way along the bench through more rocky areas. It climbs up to another bench, passes by an overhang in the bluff, and levels out a little. This overhang is big enough to get under during a rainstorm.

Not too far beyond the overhang the trail gets serious about climbing up the hillside, and does so. It switchbacks rather steeply up, then levels off for a short distance. There is a little overlook that will give you a good view of the drainage that the trail is leading up into. From here the trail heads uphill again, more switchbacks and past 76.0, up to a fairly level bench.

From this point it continues along the bench, winding its way further into the hollow, and remaining level. It eventually drops down a little and crosses a logging road. The trail works its way into the head of Waterfall Hollow, and passes underneath not one, or two, but THREE waterfalls, all of them SSSs when they are running well! The terrain in between each waterfall is easy hiking, but each time the trail turns into the hillside and heads towards the base of a waterfall the terrain gets pretty steep. Each one of these waterfalls is worthy of a stop to cool your heels at, and to enjoy their great beauty. Mile 77.0 is along the way.

After the third waterfall the trail begins to climb up the hill. It continues uphill and eventually works its way up to the top of Moonhull Mountain at 77.5, and crosses FR# 1416/CR# 9360 on a diagonal. While you are stopping to catch your breath on the way up here, you can look out onto some pretty nice views.

From the forest road the trail makes its way down into Hignite Hollow, running along one bench for a while, dropping down to the next one and so on. It continues to drop on down to and across Hignite Hollow Creek at 78.6. From there it climbs up into the woods a bit, and then intersects with a jeep road. TURN LEFT on this road, and continue up the hill.

I must pause for a moment and tell a snake story. It was at this corner one hot August day that I saw the only rattlesnake that I've ever seen on the trail. He made up for all of the rest that I missed! Five feet long would be pretty accurate. He was quite simply *huge*! But friendly — he shook his tall tail at me to let me know that he was there, then moved off a few feet to watch while I removed some old blazes and painted new ones. He had returned to "his spot" by the time that I hiked back through, and, please don't tell anybody, but I blazed him too. Now, back to the trail.

It goes *uphill*. Pretty steep in places. Fortunately, before long it tops out up on Brushy Ridge. This is a real confusing spot. There are several roads that come together here. Ignore all of them, and go STRAIGHT ahead, into the woods on trail (leave the road).

The trail drops off the hillside rapidly, and continues down, steep at times, past some giant rocks and nice big timber. It drops down to and across a small drainage, then goes up the other side, and onto a level bench. It stays here for a while, then drops down to another bench.

This bench runs right next to a stream that you can see about 100 feet below (Boomer Branch). It's a rocky trail, but very scenic and level. The bench peters out before long, and the trail climbs up to the next one. It stays on this bench for a while, passing 80.0. The trail works its way along the bench around to the nose of the ridge, then takes a nose–dive off to the left, down onto the bench below. This is a short drop, but *very* steep. And the views from this area during leaf–off are great.

The trail crosses this bench, then drops off again, down to

and across Boomer Branch at 81.0 (named after Jim Boomer, who spent his last night here). This is another one of my SSS's, and is a nice area to camp in and spend some time exploring around. Enjoy it while you can, 'cause it's a bit of a climb to get out.

The trail heads up a pretty steep grade, across a bench, then up another steep grade, then levels out a little, climbs up one last grade, and finally tops out on a fairly flat area. It passes a small wildlife opening and pond, then continues out into an open stand of timber.

As the trail crosses a log road and a clearcut area comes into view off to the right. The trail makes its way around (cut in mid 1980's), crosses another log road, then goes up and over the bank of a wildlife pond. The trail comes to one last log road.

The trail crosses the road, and for those of you interested in maps and stuff, passes a section corner marker. If you have an Ozone quad map with you, you can look at the metal plate and figure out just exactly where you are.

From here the trail rises up a little bit, working its way up and around the nose of a ridge. It remains on a level grade for a while, and offers some views out in the hills.

The trail breaks out of the woods, crosses over the flat ridgetop, then back down into the woods again. It crosses an old road, and just beyond, goes through a pile of rocks. This is a good example of the lazy man's way of clearing his field — instead of making a neat looking rock wall, this guy just piled his up in a row (sounds like something I would do). Guess he had better things to do than leave something for us to marvel at!

The trail begins to drop off a little, then breaks out over the edge of the hill, and starts a big descent down into the Mulberry River Valley. Down, down, down it switchbacks. Very nice views, but a steady, steep grade, passing 83.0 along the way. If you have weak knees like me, this will be a painful trip down. One of the things that can be seen is the hill on the opposite side. And guess what, that is where the trail goes next! Once on the bottom, the trail crosses the Mulberry River at 83.3, and then picks up a road on the opposite side.

I must pause here for a minute to tell you a bit of sad news. It was at this river crossing that a hiker died. It was on Sunday morning, November 14th, 1993. His name was James H. Boomer, a New York Supreme Court justice from Rochester. He was 71 years young, and was on day seven of his hike of the OHT. It had rained hard all weekend, and the river was swollen and running fast. Jim, an experienced hiker and noted mountain climber, attempted to cross the river, got swept away in the torrent, and drowned. As you come to this point in your hike, please observe a moment of silence in remembrance of Jim...

From the Mulberry River, follow the road on the opposite side straight ahead. There is an old tin building here on the left that some have used as a shelter. It might keep most of a downpour off, but I wouldn't spend too much time in it. The road leads just ahead to FR# 1003/CR# 5440 at 83.4. The trail crosses the road and goes up into the woods on the other side, passing under a power line.

It follows a small stream for a short distance, crosses it, and then begins a steady, *steep* climb up. This is one of the worst climbs on the trail. Take it slow, and while you are resting turn around and look at the view. About two thirds of the way up the trail leaves the roadbed that it had been following and turns to the left, going across the hillside instead of straight up it. It continues uphill, but not nearly as steep.

It levels off a bit, then climbs up a little more, and intersects an old road. TURN LEFT here, cross a small stream, and hike along a level route. Before long the trail crosses another small stream, then climbs up some more. Once on top, there is a trail intersection at 84.7. TURN RIGHT (blue blazes) and you will end up at the Ozone Trailhead Parking Lot and the end of this section. GPS 35.67296° N, -93.45064° W

If you go straight ahead at the intersection, the trail crosses Hwy. 21 and continues east, passing a spur trail that leads up to the campground.

The community of Ozone is about two miles down the highway to the right — where there is a post office and a small hamburger stand called the Red Barn (great chocolate shakes, burgers, fish, fries, and holy cow their food is great after a week on the trail! Plus you can get bottled water there since there may not be any water available at Ozone Campground).

This is the best place to resupply if you are hiking the entire trail—mail a package to yourself to the Postmaster (zip 72854). The general store at Ozone burned down a few years ago.

To keep your water bottle from freezing, keep it in the tent near you at night — it is warmer inside your tent! If you expect really cold conditions, turn your bottle upside down — it will freeze at the top first — this will keep the lid from freezing solid, and you can use what did not freeze.

SECTION FIVE — 19.1 miles
Ozone Camp TH/Hwy. 21 to Big Piney/Ft. Douglas TH

Trail Point	Mile Point	Mileage West–East	Mileage East–West
Ozone Campground TH	84.7	0.0	19.1
Little Piney River 1st cross	87.0	2.3	16.8
Little Piney River 2nd cross	88.0	3.3	15.8
FR# 1405/CR# 5550	88.3	3.6	15.5
Owens Creek	89.6	4.9	14.2
Lick Creek	92.3	7.6	11.5
Rosetta Trailhead **FR# 1004/CR# 5671**	94.3	9.6	9.5
Cedar Creek	96.5	11.8	7.3
Cedar Creek Pool	96.7	12.0	7.1
FR# 1003/CR# 5741 TH	97.9	13.2	5.9
Gee Creek	100.6	15.9	3.2
Hwy. 123	102.1	17.4	1.7
Haw Creek Falls Campground	102.4	17.7	1.4
Big Piney/Ft. Douglas TH	103.8	19.1	0.0

This 19.1 mile section begins at Ozone Campground on the Pleasant Hill Ranger District (Clarksville) and ends at the Big Piney Trailhead (now called Ft. Douglas TH by the forest service) on the Big Piney Ranger District (Hector). It passes many scenic spots, including the tallest waterfall on the trail. There are a couple of pretty good climbs along the way, but lots of nice easy hiking in between. Quad maps are Ozone, Rosetta and Fort Douglas. GPS 35.67296° N, -93.45064° W

Ozone Campground was the site of an old CCC camp during the 1930's. Some of the foundations of this camp are visible from the trail, and the site has been developed as an interpretive area. There are eight campsites here, pit toilets and *no water!* The water was so bad in the well that they had to shut it down. The campground may be closed in the winter.

 The trail begins at the trailhead parking area (84.7), which is located just across the highway from the campground entrance. There is a spur from the parking

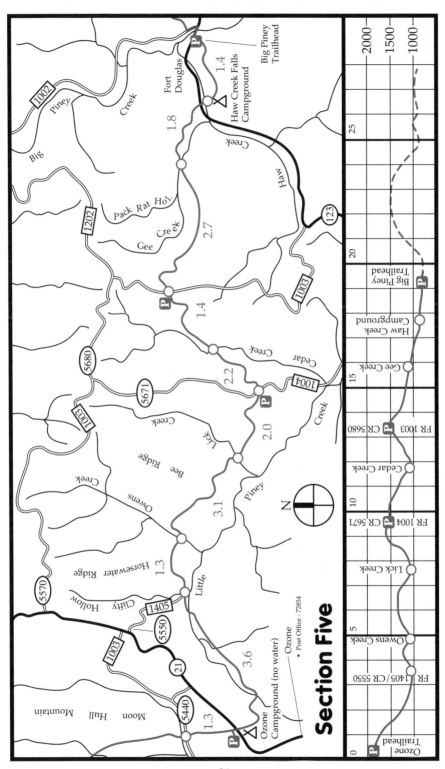

Section Five

Big Piney Trailhead

1.4

Haw Creek Falls Campground

Fort Douglas

Piney

Creek

1.8

Big

Creek

Haw

Creek

1002

1202

Pack Rat Hol.

Gee

Creek

2.7

123

1003

1.4

5680

5671

Cedar

Creek

2.2

1003

1004

P

2.0

Piney

Creek

Lick

Creek

Bee Ridge

Owens

Creek

3.1

N

5570

Horsewater Ridge

Clifty Hollow

1.3

5550

1405

Little

1003

21

Little

3.6

5440

Moon Hull Mountain

1.3

Ozone Campground (no water)

Ozone

• Post Office - 72854

P

2000

1500

1000

25

Big Piney Trailhead P

20

Haw Creek Campground

Gee Creek

15

FR 1003 CR 5680 P

Cedar Creek

10

FR 1004 CR 5671 P

Lick Creek

5

Owens Creek

FR 1405 / CR 5550

Ozone Trailhead P

0

lot that heads north and intersects with the main trail. Please be sure and register at the box. TURN RIGHT at the intersection and cross Hwy. 21. A left turn would take you back to the west on the main trail, on down to the Mulberry River.

From Hwy. 21, the trail continues into the woods and goes around the campground. You can see some of the CCC foundations off to the right (there is an interpretive trail that explores the area near the front entrance of the campground). There is an intersection with a spur trail at 84.9 that runs off up the hill to the right and goes into the back of the campground (blue blazes). The main trail goes STRAIGHT AHEAD, and begins to drop off the hill a bit, passing 85.0. From here the trail goes through some nice forest, some level, then some downhill. It switchbacks on down and through some house–sized, moss–covered boulders, then drops down to the floor of the Little Piney Creek Valley.

It hits a jeep road on the bottom and TURNS LEFT. The trail follows this road for the next couple of miles. At the beginning, it runs alongside Little Piney Creek, going downstream past 86.0. Nice easy, level walking. This is a pleasant little creek, and there are some bluffs that can be seen on the other side.

The trail passes through some good examples of rock walls, mostly off to the right. And then passes through the middle of a wildlife food plot, grown up with persimmon trees and blackberry bushes. The trail eventually crosses Little Piney Creek for the first time near 87.0. You can usually cross dry here, but during the springtime you may have to hunt for a dry crossing. Be sure and bear to the left just past the crossing.

The trail continues on this road, heading downstream. There is lots of thick brush on both sides of the trail. And even though it is always within a hundred yards of the creek, you don't see much of it. The trail crosses the creek again near 88.0. Continue on the road to the right, then straight ahead.

Soon the trail crosses an old jeep road, leaves the road and heads off into the woods. It crosses Clifty Hollow Creek, then runs uphill just a tad, and crosses FR# 1405/CR# 5550 at 88.3. If you turn left on this road, it will take you back out to Hwy. 21. If you turn right on this road, it will take you down the Little Piney Creek Valley, and come out onto Hwy. 123 after many miles.

Go STRAIGHT ACROSS this road, and up into the woods.

The trail is back to plain trail now. It works its way gradually uphill, crosses an old road, goes uphill some more, crosses another old road, then levels out a bit. It turns to the right and goes downhill through a small bluffline. It runs along a real old road bed for a while, then turns right off of it and continues out into the forest. This is all Horsewater Ridge.

The trail then crosses under a low power line and once again heads back into the woods, running level for a while. It eventually drops down a bit, then intersects with a log road and TURNS RIGHT. This old road drops down off the hill swiftly, and hits another road at the bottom. TURN LEFT on this road. The trail is only on this second road a short ways before it crosses a small stream, and then TURNS RIGHT off of the road.

The trail zig zags through the bottomland for a short distance, then crosses Owens Creek at 89.6. It goes just slightly left across the flat, then heads uphill. It switchbacks to the right then levels off a bit. It makes its way fairly level on around the nose of Bee Ridge, crosses a jeep road, then drops down into and across a small drainage.

It switchbacks its way up the hill, kind of following that small creek. The trail is rather steep in places here. This section has been rerouted around a clearcut. It continues up, then eventually levels off, and turns more to the right. Still on the level, it crosses a small drainage, then comes out into a cedar glade and goes straight across it, then continues into the woods.

The trail stays level for a while, then drops a little, down to an old roadbed. It follows this roadbed for a while, crosses a small drainage, and then TURNS RIGHT off of the roadbed just after the drainage. It remains level, then drops down to and across a jeep road, then continues level again.

The trail weaves its way through some giant rocks with some bluffs nearby, then drops down into and across a rocky stream, full of waterfalls and dreams at 91.6, another one of my SSS's.

From here the trail stays level, works its way around a point, then begins to drop off a little, and crosses an old road. Beyond the road it descends quickly down into the Lick Creek drainage. As you go down you can look across the valley and see a hill that looms larger with each step — yep, we're going up it next!

But first the trail switchbacks down the hill into the bottom, where it crosses Lick Creek at 92.3 (the creek that you crossed at the beginning of this section is Lick *Branch*). Once on the other side the trail turns to the left, uphill, and crosses a jeep road. The trail continues across this road, running up the hill on an old roadbed. But first, let me tell about one of my special places.

Instead of crossing this road, turn left on it. Go about 300 yards. On the left and just down the hill you will find "Slot Rock," a place that I found and named many years ago. There is a large slab rock that spans the entire creek here. The water has cut a "slot" into it, and with the ledge that the rock forms, creates a neat waterfall into a wonderful pool. This pool, although small, is usually six or seven feet deep! The slab rock all around has some carved out places just perfect for a tired body to lie down on and soak up some rays. A very special place to spend a few hours. This is not a good place to camp though — not enough flat area. *Please keep this area*, as well as the rest of the trail, *spotless!*

Ahhh, what a refreshing break. Now back to the trail. Cross the road and head up the hill on another old road. And I do mean UP the hill. This is another bad climb. Up it goes, then level, then up again. Then the road peters out and you are on pure trail again, and again going up. But not for long. Soon it levels out, and then actually drops down a bit and comes alongside a small stream.

Here, there is an intersection at 92.9. Turn right for a spur trail (blue blazes) that goes down to Bear Skull Falls (class D, 22'). If you are from Arkansas, and are familiar with Cedar Falls at Petit Jean State Park, this falls and the rock formations around it may remind you of Cedar Falls — of course on a much smaller scale. When running, this is a great little diversion.

Back at the intersection, TURN LEFT and go uphill for the main trail. It makes its way around the falls area up a steep grade. It levels off and then comes to another intersection. Again turn right to another, smaller falls, but TURN LEFT for the main trail.

It continues uphill, then level, then up again, and across a log road. The trail swings to the right, easing up the hill, levels a bit, then curves back to the right and levels off.

The trail passes just above a nice little SSS waterfall, then swings back to the left, then right, then back left again, all uphill.

It tops out pretty much for good through a saddle, and runs along the side of the hill and through several tiny drains. You'll pass a very small spring-fed pond on the right—*always* water here—an SSS spot worth a rest stop, especially on hot days.

The trail continues mostly on the level, in and out of several tiny drains, then begins to work its way downhill, joining an old road trace at one point, then comes out to a small parking area called Rosetta Trailhead on FR# 1004/CR# 5671 at 94.3. Cross this forest road and head out into the woods, bearing to the left.

The trail wanders around through the woods, gradually making its way downhill, dropping off onto benches below. On one downhill grade, the trail is on an old roadbed. It stays on this roadbed for a while, then makes a sharp right turn.

Soon after this turn, the trail leaves the roadbed and TURNS LEFT. Here it lands on a nice level bench that you will stay on for a while. It runs along the edge of a steep dropoff, and the views down into the Cedar Creek valley are great. Except for the ridge that you can see on the other side — the trail climbs up that in a couple of miles.

The trail becomes an old roadbed again and continues along this bench, on a nice level route. It crosses a rocky drainage and then leaves the roadbed TO THE RIGHT. It goes over to the steep edge that I mentioned and goes down *over* the edge! There are lots of rock steps here — be careful when it's wet or frozen.

Once down this steep grade the trail turns right, then left, and drops down onto another bench. Here it picks up another old road and follows it along the same bench for quite a while. This is another really pleasant walking section. Fairly level. And lots of big trees. White oak, black gum, sweet gum and a bunch of big beeches! One of the best stands of beeches in the Forest.

The trail eventually leaves the roadbed to the right, heads out across the bench and heads downhill.

There is a small canyon that you can see off to the left as you descend. If you have the time, this is a nice little area to explore, especially during the wet season where you will find Hobo Falls East (23') and Hobo Falls West (27'). While hunting waterfalls one day I found what appeared to be an abandoned hobo camp behind one of the falls, therefore Hobo Falls.

Once the trail gets off the hill, it turns right, following the creek that comes out of Hobo Canyon (why not?). Then it crosses that creek (Hobo Creek?), and then crosses Cedar Creek at 96.5. From here the trail bumps up a small bench and intersects with a jeep road. TURN LEFT and continue on the road. It goes up a bench, then levels out for a while.

The trail then leaves this roadbed TO THE LEFT. Right here, off on the flat area to the right of the road, is a great place to camp. Lots of level area, and a fire ring. Please always camp on the east side of this road when in this area. The trail swings to the left then to the right out to an overlook of another one of the great spots on the trail at 96.7. In fact there is about a twenty foot spur trail here that takes you to the overlook.

This is a beautiful pool, always emerald green it seems, with the creek spilling right into it. Of course it is an SSS. A word of caution — the pool is not very deep — not deep enough to jump into. OK for a swim sure, but wade into it from downstream. Also, be sure and don't camp near the pool — the vegetation is just too fragile here. Go back to where I just mentioned for a fine camp spot.

From this little spur the trail continues on, hits the old roadbed for just a few feet, then crosses a slippery rock ledge. This is *always* slippery, so be careful. Just across this ledge the trail swings to the right and heads uphill. It soon heads back to the left, then right again, and levels off.

This next section of trail is basically a long, steady, rocky, steep climb up. A few level spots, but not too many. It eventually makes its way up to and around the nose of a ridge, leveling off. There is a great view of the valley and hills beyond from here.

The trail keeps climbing, but more gradually, to where you can see ahead and up, a low spot or "saddle" in the ridge—that is where the trail is heading. In the meantime, the trail crosses a small creek, and there are class B waterfalls both uphill and downhill. It levels out a little, then drops down to and crosses another stream with a class B waterfall below.

From here, it climbs gradually, through another drainage, then up into a real rocky area. It bends around to the right, still climbing a little, and then finally comes into the saddle that I just mentioned. It levels out and comes to a small parking area at FR# 1003/CR# 5741 at 97.9, then crosses it.

From FR# 1003 the trail levels off a bit past 98.0, and runs through a dense thicket, and enters the Big Piney Ranger District

(Hector). There is a switchback as you start the descent down to Gee Creek. You'll get a good view of the surrounding hills on the way down. The trail is well contoured, not too steep.

Once in the bottom, the trail crosses several small creeks and goes past 100.0. There are lots of places to stop for the night. Gee Creek is forded at about 100.6. Just east of this crossing the trail goes through a clearcut area, then heads back into the woods. This would be a good spot to camp — there is a rock wall next to the creek, with a great view into the clearcut area. You are likely to see some deer browsing or other wildlife.

The trail climbs up a little, looks down on Gee Creek, and crosses several nice little streams on its way to Hwy. 123. There are some large pine trees throughout this area. The trail comes down off the hill, passes a trail register (be sure and sign in), and hits paved Hwy. 123 at 102.1 at the turnoff to Haw Creek Falls Campground.

To get to the campground and the continuation of the trail, go straight ahead here, across the highway and past a gate. The first thing you will have to do is cross Haw Creek. It is very wide, and you usually have to get a little wet to cross.

Note that the campground is often closed during the winter (not the trail though), and also might be gated if the creek is high. If you find flooded conditions you can bypass the creek by turning left at the highway and hike about a mile along Highway 123 to the Big Piney/Ft. Douglas Trailhead where you can pick up the trail again.

Haw Creek Falls Campground is a small Forest Service campground, and one of my favorites in the Forest. There are usually very few folks that use this area, but it can get crowded on popular weekends. One of the main attractions is the falls on the river — accessible via a short trail just across from the toilets. The falls are a small class B, but nice. In fact, the upper part is a large, flat rock bed — perfect for stretching out for a well–deserved snooze! It's a great spot for moondipping.

There is a fee for camping here (Big Piney Ranger District, Hector). The water is OK (I'd rather drink filtered water out of the creek though), and the campground is sometimes closed during the winter, and during high water! (see note above)

By the way, you might be wondering about "Gee" and "Haw." They are old timers' directions — "*Gee*" means "right," and "*Haw*" means "left." Gee Creek runs into Haw Creek, and if you were standing right there, Haw Creek would be to your "left," and Gee Creek would be to your "right." So there, now you know some hillbilly talk!

Once you get to the campground the trail follows the road through the campground and leaves out the back of the campground as normal trail. It crosses a creekbed that is often dry. If you camp here and have some time to kill, hike up this little hollow — there are some really nice waterfalls and rock formations further up, including the now famous Pack Rat Falls.

The trail heads up on the side of the hill, climbing gradually, and looks down on Haw Creek. This is a pretty little section. Not too steep, and it levels off shortly. There is a huge sandstone boulder next to the trail about a half mile from the campground that kind of reminds me of my high school Geometry teacher.

Shortly after this rugged looking character, the trail runs on an old road, and crosses a small drainage. Then the trail leaves the roadbed to THE RIGHT, and becomes trail again.

A quarter mile down the trail you cross FR# 1002/CR# 5861, continue down the hill, and across a grown–up field. This field ends up as the Big Piney/Ft Douglas Trailhead parking at 103.8. Adjacent to the lot is the old Fort Douglas School House. This is the end of section five. GPS 35.67790° N, -93.23812° W

A good way to take toilet paper with you on the trail is to carry one of those travel packs of Kleenex tissues. You can get a bundle of them for next to nothing, and always have them handy. A note of caution though — it is not a good idea to use white toilet paper during deer season! (When in use, white toilet paper has a way of resembling the tail or "flag" of a whitetail deer running away. I've often heard a hunter remark that all they got was a shot at a "flag." Not a very good way to go!)

If you get cold at night, try covering your sleeping bag with your raincoat or poncho — it will help retain your heat and keep you warmer. Put on a stocking cap too (or wear a hooded sweatshirt). And munch on a candy bar or other sweet treat — this will stoke your fire.

When you bend down to tie your shoe/boot, always tie the other one too. If not, as soon as you start hiking again, the other one will feel loose and bug you 'till you stop again to tie it. Doing both at the same time will save you time and the effort of bending down twice.

If you can afford the room/weight, carry a separate pot just for boiling water. You won't ever have to wash it! This works great with a two–person cook group. I carry a tiny pot when hiking solo too that doesn't weigh much.

And speaking of pots and cooking, if you really want to squeeze as much cooking time out of your gas as you can, paint your pots black — they will heat up faster. Use a can of oven paint.

Ziplocks, ziplocks, ziplocks. There are literally hundreds of uses for these. But you can never think of them all. Carry a couple of small and large ones in your pack — you will usually find something that they are just perfect for.

Keeping an accurate equipment list — and maintaining it faithfully after every trip — will help you fine tune your pack. Make a list of everything that you take on your trip. When you get home, sit down with the list and scratch off anything that you did not use (as well as adding things that you needed). Some items, like a first aid kit, should always be carried though, even if you don't use it. Eventually, you will have pared down the weight of your pack so that you don't feel the need for a sherpa!

SECTION SIX — 20.0 miles
Big Piney/Ft. Douglas Trailhead to Fairview Trailhead/Hwy. 7

Trail Point	Mile Point	Mileage West–East	Mileage East–West
Big Piney/Ft. Douglas TH	103.8	0.0	20.0
Wilderness Boundary	104.1	.3	19.7
Highwater Bypass Trail	107.8	4.0	16.0
Hurricane Cr., west cross	109.4	5.6	14.4
Natural Bridge	109.9	6.1	13.9
Greasy Creek	112.0	8.2	11.8
Hurricane Cr., east cross	113.4	9.6	10.4
Spur Trail to Chancel	116.9	13.1	6.9
Chancel Trailhead	**116.9 + .6 spur**	**13.7**	**7.5**
Wilderness Boundary	117.4	13.6	6.4
Unnamed Creek	119.5	15.7	4.3
4-wheeler rd./Buck Br.	121.8	18.0	2.0
Fairview Trailhead/Hwy. 7	123.8	20.0	0.0

This 20 mile section of trail connects two Forest Service trailheads, and passes through one of the most scenic spots in Arkansas — the Hurricane Creek Wilderness Area. One of the highlights of this area is the huge natural rock bridge there. And of course Hurricane Creek itself is just terrific — full of boulders and pool after pool of gorgeous water. Big Piney Ranger District (Hector). Quad maps are Fort Douglas and Sand Gap. GPS 35.67790° N, -93.23812° W

The trailhead is located between Clarksville and Pelsor on paved Hwy. 123 (a nice drive from either direction), just east of Haw Creek Falls Campground and near the Big Piney River (great floating stream).

From the parking lot, the trail TURNS RIGHT (east) on Hwy. 123 and crosses Big Piney River on a steel bridge. This bridge was constructed in 1931. The Big Piney river here is usually a pretty green color. The area under the bridge is a good catfish and swimming hole. Upstream a mile or so is also great smallmouth fishing.

When you get to the east end of the bridge, TURN LEFT (north) on FR# 1002/CR#5881 and pass 104.0. A couple hundred

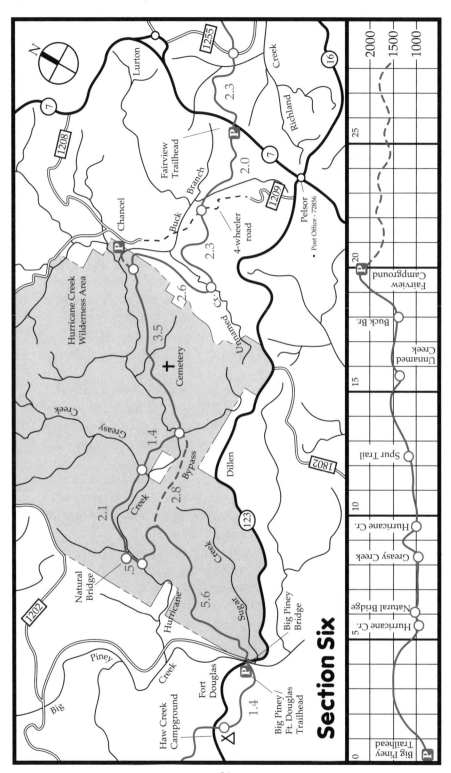

Section Six

Lurton

1255

Creek

16

1208

7

Fairview
Trailhead

2.3

Buck   Branch

P

7

Chancel

2.0

1209

4-wheeler
road

2.3

Pelsor
• Post Office - 72856

P

Hurricane Creek
Wilderness Area

2.6

Unnamed Cr.

3.5

+
Cemetery

Greasy   Creek

1.4

Bypass

Dillen

1802

2.1

Creek

2.8

123

.5

Natural
Bridge

Hurricane

Creek

Sugar   Creek

5.6

Big Piney
Bridge

1202

Piney

Creek

Fort
Douglas

Big

Haw Creek
Campground

P

1.4

Big Piney /
Ft. Douglas
Trailhead

N

2000

1500

1000

25

P 20
Fairview Campground

Buck Br.

Unnamed Creek

15

Spur Trail

10

Hurricane Cr.

Greasy Creek

Natural Bridge

5

Hurricane Cr.

0

Big Piney Trailhead P

yards down this road at 104.1 the trail leaves the road up a small flight of steps TO THE RIGHT. This is the boundary for the 15,000–acre Hurricane Creek Wilderness Area, which was designated in 1984. There is a trail register here, so be sure and sign up. While you are in the Wilderness Area, the paint blazes will be farther apart — to help keep more of the wilderness character. Mountain bikes are not allowed.

The trail crosses a small stream, and heads up the hill. You should *fill up with water here* — the next reliable supply is Hurricane Creek, five miles away. During the dry months, fill up at Big Piney.

The next half mile plus, I'm afraid to tell you, is uphill. Along the way, you'll find a nice bluffline just below the trail off to the right. If you have the time, and it's good to stop and rest going up anyway, veer over and hang around the bluffs a moment or two. The view down into the Sugar Creek drainage is nice.

The trail continues to climb, turns back to the left, then swings right past 106.0 and tops out over the hill. It levels off, then eases up a small bench.

The next mile of trail is a nice level walk through a beech forest. Soon the trail leaves the old roadbed it has been following TO THE RIGHT. There is some evidence of tornado damage in this area. It continues on, running level, then makes a gradual swing to the left.

At about 107.8 there is a trail intersection and sign. Turn right and you'll be taking the high–water bypass trail (marked with blue blazes). This bypass trail goes 2.8 miles across the hillside and drops down to rejoin the main trail at 113.4.

Use the bypass trail to avoid having to cross Hurricane Creek twice if water levels are high, otherwise, turn LEFT at the sign (actually straight ahead). The main trail runs across wide open level forest, through some nice big white oaks past 108.0, then turns back to the west and begins the descent down to Hurricane Creek. The trail goes into an SSS of rock outcrops, then continues swithbacking down past 109.0 to the first/west of two crossings of Hurricane Creek at 109.5.

This crossing is never a good one. Plan on wading. It's not too deep, but the bottom is *very slick*. You probably need a walking stick or sturdy limb here. Also, a pair of socks will help a great deal with the slippery bottom. The view both up and downstream is really nice from this crossing. The trail resumes across the river and takes off up the hill.

It climbs up a bit and comes out onto an old pioneer road, TURNS RIGHT and levels off. *Be alert to this turn if going west—it is easy to miss!* (You used to be able to exit the wilderness area by taking this pioneer road back to the east here for two miles, however it is now blocked by private property near the end, and the land owner does not allow hikers to cross his land—it is to be used for dire emergencies only!)

Heading east on this old pioneer road will take you quickly past a gorgeous bluff off to the left. Once you find the bluff, watch for a "Bridge" sign again on the left, a couple of hundred yards from the start of the bluffline at 109.9. Hike up to the base of the bluff and look UP—at the top of the bluffline is the Hurricane Creek Natural Bridge. All of this area an SSS—both the bridge and the bluff are spectacular!

Back down on the ground, as a last resort you could camp under this bluffline — there is lots of room, and many have done it. I don't recommend it though, except in case of emergency, 'cause I've heard a lot of "bear stories" from those who do.

From the bridge, the trail continues down the pioneer road, turns sharp right, then sharp left, past 110.0. At the first turn, you'll be looking right into a house–sized boulder. It is sitting in Cedar Limb Hollow. This is one of the most spectacular scenic areas in this part of the country. You need to spend some time here. There are lots of waterfalls, all sizes, huge beech trees, and lots and lots of giant boulders and tall bluffs upstream.

Wildman Falls is up in this area. It is named after Carl "The Wildman" Ownbey, a longtime OHTA member. He and I had just packed a bunch of heavy camera equipment into this area (I was making a film of the Wilderness Area), when we both sat down to rest. We had a large slug of whiskey. When Carl stood up, it all went to his head I guess, and he collapsed and fell head first off of the rocks we were sitting on. He hit the rocks below pretty hard. I was afraid that I would have to carry him out. Fortunately, after a couple of hours rest next to "his" waterfall, he was able to move again, and eventually hike out.

Carl hiked more miles than anyone I ever knew, including all of the OHT several times, the entire Appalachian Trail (2,000 miles plus), and the entire Continental Divide Trail from Canada to Mexico (3,000 miles plus!)—and he didn't even begin hiking until he was in his 60's! The Wildman kept on hiking well into his 80's before going to the great trail in the sky. Think about Carl when you are moaning about being too old to hike.

Back up on the OHT, if you continue to the second turn you'll be looking at Hurricane Creek again, and just off to the right is the most popular camping spot in the area. Down on the creek is one of my favorite SSS's — a large, flat rock that sticks out into the creek. Again, the view both up and downstream is wonderful. I have spent many hours here just looking, contemplating, wishing. Just downstream is a good swimming hole. And the "orange" color that you see on the giant boulder just downstream isn't paint, it's lichen.

The biggest problem with this camp spot, and the immediate area in general, is the fact that there isn't much level room to set up tents. There is only room for four or five tents. This is probably a blessing in disguise! There is not enough room for large groups.

Back up on the pioneer road, continue down it and you'll cross a small stream—this is Cedar Limb Hollow that I just spoke of. Just across it is the rockiest road I ever saw! Guess this is where the ice cream comes from.

The trail pretty much follows Hurricane Creek upstream for a while. There are terrific views of the creek with each step. There are a couple of good, small campsites too.

The trail leaves the pioneer road and rolls gently along in the woods beside the creek. If you are quiet, you may spot a beaver working this area in the evening. The trail returns to the road then turns north and heads up Greasy Creek valley. You'll notice some rock walls, and even a chimney here, just before you cross Greasy Creek at 111.99.

You should cross Greasy Creek just upstream from where the road crosses it, then back on the road again and pass 112.0. Soon you'll leave the road, and the easy hiking, and head TO THE LEFT, up the hill. At this point there may be a trail going straight ahead. This leads into some private property called "The Valley Of Light," which was owned by a rather religious person. It seems that he moved his followers here decades ago to await the end of the world.

Just across Hurricane Creek upstream from this property several friends from the Sierra Club own some acreage called

Murkwood. They have moved an old log cabin onto the place—a wonderful location for a log cabin. The trail doesn't really go near their place, but you may get a glimpse of it from the forthcoming hill.

Like I said, the trail turns left and heads uphill, at times rather steeply, and makes its way through a tornado area. Once on top, the view up and down the Hurricane Creek valley (and Greasy Creek too) is magnificent. The knocked down trees from the tornado provided room for the view (until they grow up).

The descent back into the Hurricane Creek Valley is gentle, passing 113.0. You arrive at the bottom next to a nice, tall rock chimney at 113.8, and intersect with the road that goes into the private property.

TURN LEFT and hike down the road a few hundred feet to the second/east crossing of Hurricane Creek at 113.4. Unfortunately, this is another wade–the–creek situation, and the water can get up to waist deep. Usually it's only knee deep or less, but may be kind of slick. Go across the creek on the road, but TURN OFF THE ROAD TO THE RIGHT a hundred feet beyond. Another hundred feet or so of trail will bring you to an intersection — the highwater bypass trail will come down from the right and rejoin (blue blazes). Be sure to TURN LEFT here.

The trail from here generally just heads upstream, back off in the woods a ways, and rolls up and down through the forest past 114.0. There has been a lot of tornado damage in this area, but the trail corridor has always been cleared quickly by volunteers.

At about 114.6 you'll cross a usable road. This road goes up a *steep* hill to the right a ways to an old cemetery. This road, and the one that goes to the private property you were on are still used. How can this be you say, isn't this a *Wilderness* Area? Yes it is, but all landowners in a wilderness area are allowed vehicle access, and the county judge in addition has opened this road to anyone who wants to visit the cemetery. It's an unusual deal. So if you see a car in this wilderness area, don't get too upset. Chances are they are supposed to be there.

As you hike along you'll have some great views, then the trail drops off the hill and comes alongside Hurricane Creek again. At 116.9 there is a trail intersection with a sign. If you turned left (blue blazes), you'd come out at the Chancel Trailhead in about .6. There is a gorgeous rock wall along part of this little–used spur. **Note** that you have to ford Hurricane Creek to the trailhead by car or by foot.

TURN RIGHT at this intersection and continue on the main trail. It climbs gradually up and around the ridge. As you come around this ridge, you'll have a wonderful view, and will also be looking right down on top of a house. This is Chancel (or used to be). As you cross an old road on this ridge at 117.4, you will leave the Wilderness Area.

From this point you will climb gradually again, for about half a mile, up several rocky benches, and will be heading back to the south. The flat bench that you finally land on has several "boulder fields" that the trail goes right through. Don't worry if you can't really see the trail here — just keep going straight ahead, and you'll come out to it.

There are a couple of spots in this area where the trail leaves an apparent road bed, so be alert. The trail drops down to and crosses an unnamed stream at 119.5, then heads up the other side, heading back to the north. About 250 feet past the creek the trail leaves the road bed and TURNS LEFT into the woods.

As the trail continues there is some more tornado damage from years ago. There are also some giant boulders around the 120.5 area—you will see a lot of them, an entire rock garden! This immediate area is one of my favorites on the trail, an SSS. At one point the trail actually goes under one of the large boulders. Back up on the hillside, there is a wonderful bluffline that goes for quite a ways. There are lots of places to get out of the rain if you need to.

Back in 1980 I had to do just that while on a hike across America with HikaNation. In fact, I spent a couple of hours under one of these rocks with famed outdoorsman Jim Rawlins of North Little Rock. We were quite a ways ahead of the group, and soaked to the bone. The fire we built helped warm and dry out nearly 50 hikers that day. I don't think that any of them appreciated our cold December rain!

Once you leave the boulder area the trail winds its way down a 4-wheeler road, and Buck Branch Creek. TURN RIGHT on the road, and follow it (across a small bridge) for about 600 feet. Then TURN LEFT and continue down an old log road. *Be alert if traveling west* to these intersections.

The trail crosses a small creek, and 300 feet later leaves the roadbed and TURNS LEFT. This begins the two–mile climb up to the Fairview Trailhead, past 122.0 and 123.0. The climb is fairly gradual, with lots of nearly level walking. One area goes through a large stand of pines to the right, and looks down to the left onto Buck Branch.

You will top out on the level and come to a short spur trail at 123.8—TURN RIGHT to get to the Fairview Trailhead parking area. This is the end of Section Six. GPS 35.73875° N, -93.09376° W

There was once a fire tower at this campground, with nothing but tiny pine trees as far as you could see. Since then, the tower was taken down, the trees grew up, and the campground was built. Now the campground has been closed due to budget cuts. So sad. But the last time I was there a couple of camp spots, a vault toilet, and water remained for use by hikers.

The Pelsor Post Office is just over a mile down the highway. The old Hankins General Store there has closed down and until it reopens with new ownership cannot be relied on for resupply. Hwy. 7 is, by the way, a National Scenic Byway, and considered one of the most scenic drives in the United States.

The woods are full of dish rags — use a handful of dead leaves to wipe out your dishes, then toss the leaves into the campfire. Rinse with a little water, then repeat. Do a final wipe with a towel if needed.

Mini Mag flashlights have a spare bulb hidden behind the spring in the rear section. Just pull out the spring and you'll find it. Also, if you unscrew the front of these lights completely, and they will act like a lantern, casting a broad beam of light (hang from the roof of your tent).

SECTION SEVEN — 19.3 miles
Fairview Campground (Hwy. 7) to Richland Creek Camp

Trail Point	Mile Point	Mileage West–East	Mileage East–West
Fairview Trailhead/Hwy. 7	123.8	0.0	19.3
FR# 1255/CR# 5000	126.1	2.3	17.0
Cox Hollow	127.6	3.8	15.5
Greenhaw Hollow	129.3	5.5	13.8
Unnamed Hollow	130.4	6.6	12.7
Moore CCC Camp	133.0	9.2	10.1
Moore CCC access parking	133.0 + .6 spur	9.8	10.7
Richland Creek	133.2	9.4	9.9
Ben Hur/Moore Trailhead	134.5	10.6	8.7
FR# 1203/CR# 5050	135.0	11.2	8.1
Falling Water Creek	138.4	14.6	4.7
Richland Cr. Campground	143.1	19.3	0.0

This 19.3 mile section connects an old Forest Service campground (Fairview Campground, which is no longer open for camping), with the Richland Creek Campground, both located on the Big Piney Ranger District (Hector). There aren't any real spectacular areas in this section, but there is a lot of nice country, and several scenic spots. It crosses both Richland Creek and Falling Water Creek, but it bypasses one of the most scenic areas in the state — Richland Creek Wilderness Area. Quad maps are Sand Gap, Lurton and Moore. GPS 35.73875° N -93.09376° W

The Fairview Trailhead is located on Scenic Hwy. 7 (a National Scenic Byway). There is water, a pit toilet, and a couple of old campsites for hikers, but no official camping. About a mile south of the trailhead is the community of Pelsor. It has a Post Office (zip 72856), but that is about it. The old Hankins General Store there may or may not be open (varies from year to year, and by season), depending on ownership. When the store is open they have snacks, drinks, and sandwiches, and has lots of historic artifacts—but don't count on restocking your pack with backpacking food.

The trailhead is well marked along Hwy. 7—just pull in and turn right, then the road will end at the trailhead.

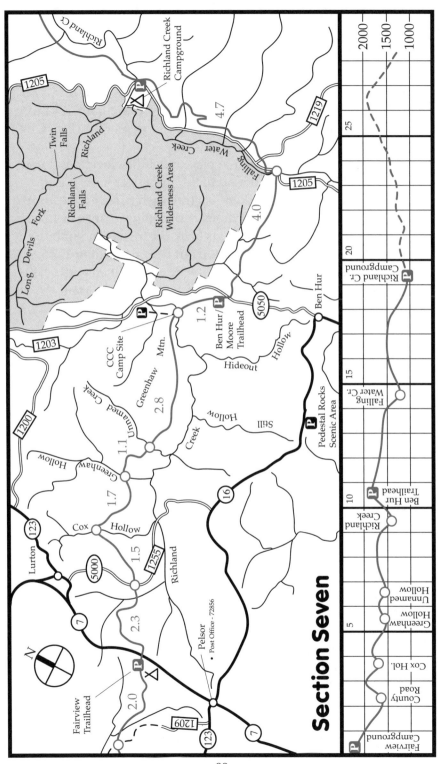

Section Seven

Richland Cr.

1205

Twin Falls

Richland

Richland Falls

Long Devils Fork

Richland Creek Wilderness Area

Richland Creek Campground

P

4.7

Falling Water Creek

1219

1205

1203

CCC Camp Site

P

Greenhaw Mtn.

2.8

1.2

Ben Hur / Moore Trailhead

P

5050

Hideout

Hollow

Ben Hur

Unnamed Creek

1.1

Creek

Still Hollow

Pedestal Rocks Scenic Area

P

16

1200

Greenhaw Hollow

1.7

Cox Hollow

1.5

1255

Richland

Lurton 123

5000

2.3

Pelsor
Post Office - 72856

N

Fairview Trailhead

P

2.0

1209

123

7

7

2000
1500
1000

25

20

Richland Cr. Campground

P

15

Falling Water Cr.

10

Ben Hur Trailhead

P

Richland Creek

Unnamed Hollow

Greenhaw Hollow

5

Cox Hol.

County Road

Fairview Campground

P

66

The trail leaves the back end of the trailhead (123.8) to the north and crosses Hwy. 7. It heads out through a fairly open hardwood forest past 124.0 and 125.0, gradually losing elevation. It turns back to the east and drops off the hill, following a small drainage into the bottomland. It's fairly level for a while, crosses a creek, and then crosses FR# 1255/CR# 5000 at 126.1.

From this point, you begin to pick up a little elevation. If you notice a red blazed tree down off to the right near here, it is a private property corner marker. The trail then passes 127.0, drops off the hill again down to and across Cox Hollow Creek at 127.6.

Across the creek the trail heads back upstream, and uphill. It's a pretty good climb, but you top out before reaching 128.8. The trail passes another private property corner, then goes through a "saddle" (low spot between two hills). The trail descends past 129.0 and into Greenhaw Hollow.

Once in the bottom, you pick up a real nice, thick cedar thicket, and follow through it about a 1,000 feet, exiting at Greenhaw Hollow creek at 129.3. The crossing is on a slab rock that makes up the entire stream bottom. You can usually cross dry by going upstream 100 feet or so. Once again the trail climbs quickly up, but not for long. You pass an old chimney (could this be that of Mr. Greenhaw?) in a pine grove. From here the trail heads downhill again. At this point be careful — the path crosses/runs along a narrow roadbed several times.

The trail crosses an unnamed creek, then heads uphill onto Greenhaw Mountain and the going is easy on past 131.0. The trail winds on around fairly level until you pass a large pine plantation off to the right (south). The trail begins its descent to Richland Creek and follows just under this plantation. The trail then wraps around to the edge of the ridge, and you have a terrific view up and down the valley.

The trail begins to pass through the area where the old Moore CCC camp was located. Near 133.0 you come out to a trailhead register, and an old road. This is a good time to stop and spend an hour or so looking at all the ruins of the camp. This was the end of the OHT for many years.

TURN RIGHT on the road and follow it around for a couple of hundred feet. On your left is the rock and concrete remains of some sort of building, I'm not sure just what, but it looks like it could prove a good shelter — though the floor is too clean to be totally dry! Just past this ruins, the trail leaves the road TO THE RIGHT, and drops down to Richland Creek at 133.2.

[There is a small "unofficial" parking area and spur trail to an access point where you can park to access the trail or the historical CCC camp, especially useful if Richland Creek is flooded. Go straight on this road noted above for .6 miles (follow blue blazes around private property). The parking area is just off FR# 1203/CR# 5050. There is a bridge across Richland Creek on the road if you needed to bypass the trail crossing due to high water.]

The Wilderness Area is a mile or more downstream, but the water here is gorgeous! I should make a note here about the Wilderness Area. There is no finer section of land in the country than the Richland Creek Wilderness Area. It is simply the best there is. But, Forest Service regulations prohibit cross–country trails from being built through wilderness areas, so the next 10 miles of trail bypasses the wilderness area. It's a shame to miss such wonderful country, but then maybe there will be less traffic in the wilderness area and more for us to enjoy without a trail. By the way, the trail was already located through Hurricane Creek Wilderness before it became wilderness area. Good thing!

After you've dried your shoes, the trail will take you up, up and away from the Richland valley. You start off following a small stream, then take off up the hill. You cross the stream, get on an old road, and climb further — pretty steep in places. Once you pass 134.0, you're through the worst of it. The trail passes a registration box, and comes out at the Ben Hur/Moore Trailhead at 134.6 (not to be confused with "Moore CCC" Trailhead). To reach this trailhead, turn north on FR# 1203/CR# 5050 at the community of Ben Hur (on paved Hwy. 16), follow the road a little over a mile, then turn left on FR# 1203D. It will take you right to the parking lot. This last stretch of road can be a mess when it gets wet. GPS 134.535.75371° N, -92.98234° W

From the parking lot, cross the road and head into the woods. The trail is mostly level for a while and passes 135.0 just before it crosses FR# 1203/CR# 5050 and goes under a power line. Then the trail dips a bit, crosses a small stream, then wanders around through the forest mostly level. The trail turns north a little, then turns back to the east past 136.0 and climbs. You will notice an open field off to the south — private property.

At 136.6 you cross a jeep road, and the trail levels off and passes under another powerline. Just beyond here the trail runs up onto a small pond bank. This is one of many water holes that are built by the Arkansas Game and Fish Commission to help wildlife during dry periods.

The trail picks up an old roadbed just beyond the pond and follows it for a while, passing next to that powerline again. Then it crosses another jeep road, and you begin to descend into the Falling Water Creek Valley. There are a few confusing spots here so be alert for the trail.

The trail falls off the hill quickly, then swings around to the north and you enter a lovely area of large pine trees, huge boulders, with a great view up and down the valley, an SSS. Then the trail switchbacks several times to the south, through many boulders, down to and across a boulder–strewn stream. There is a great bluffline in this area too.

The trail continues down the hill, on and off an old log road, swings back to the left and crosses the creek again near the bottom. Just past this crossing, the trail crosses a horse trail and just beyond that it comes out on FR# 1205/Falling Water Road— TURN LEFT on the road and cross the bridge that spans Falling Water Creek at 138.4.

For waterfall lovers, that horse trail goes 1.0 to the famous "Fuzzybutt Falls" and access to other waterfalls along the way.

Once across the bridge TURN LEFT and follow the creek downstream. This is a neat SSS area along the creek, but soon the trail leaves the creek to the right, crosses FR# 1205, heads up into the woods, crosses under another powerline, then FR# 1219.

The next four miles of trail pretty much follows to the east and just uphill of FR# 1205. During the winter you can see the road (and Falling Water Creek) below most of the time. There long vistas along the way, and lots of rock outcrops and bluffs just above the trail.

There is an unofficial spur trail to the right near 139.9 that goes .5 mile up a side creek to the 78' tall Keefe Falls. In fact almost every drainage in this area has a waterfall or two upstream at the bluffline—best to explore during winter.

By the way, the forest road below forms the eastern boundary of the Richland Creek Wilderness, so all of the country that you are looking at across the road is **Wilderness**! And this 12,000–acre tract is some of the most scenic backcountry we have.

Be on the lookout at 141.0 where the trail TURNS RIGHT and switchbacks steeply UP the hillside, perhaps the steepest part of the entire OHT. It soon levels off and works its way around and above Landslide Falls, which will be below the trail out of sight. This mile+ up high is a re-route around a landslide that in 2008 removed a large part of the hill, as you will see. The views from up there are amazing, but there is also a bluffline below so be very careful!

The re-route crosses a small creek that feeds the waterfall, then goes up to the left, then swings around to the right, passing above some of those blufflines—all of this area is an SSS! Eventually the trail winds around the landslide and past 142.0 and down the hill to level out again and turn right back onto the original trail.

Near 142.7 the trail switchbacks down around the hill to the right, comes into a pine/cedar grove, and passes 143.0. It runs down the hill a little more and arrives at the entrance to Richland Creek Campground and FR# 1205 at 143.1 and is the end of section seven. GPS 35.79649° N, -92.93826°W

The campground is a small one, with a few tables, a pit toilet and a well.

If you have the chance, I would definitely recommend spending at least a day in the Richland Wilderness. You can camp at the campground and dayhike if you want to. Just head up Richland from the campground — the most scenic part is the first four miles.

*When you put your sleeping bag and tent away in their stuff sacks, you should do just that — **stuff them!** Yes, even the tent. It won't hurt it a bit, and in fact will keep from creating creases that weaken the material if you rolled it the same way each time. An added benefit to stuffing your fluffed–up bag into that tiny stuff sack is that on chilly mornings the extra effort needed helps warm you up! Try to get the bottom half of the bag into the bottom half of the stuff sack. Also, when you get home, take the bag out of the stuff sack and store it loose, which will keep the insulating material from compressing.*

SECTION EIGHT — 20.9 miles
Richland Creek Campground to Buffalo River (Woolum)

Trail Point	Mile Point	Mileage West–East	Mileage East–West
Richland Creek Campground Entrance	143.1	0.0	20.9
Richland Creek crossing #1	143.2	.1	20.8
Long Branch	145.4	2.3	18.6
Drury Hollow	146.7	3.6	17.3
Armstrong Hollow	147.5	4.4	16.5
Stack Rock TH/FR#1201	150.8	7.7	13.2
Spur to Stack Rock Falls	151.4	8.3	12.6
Dry Creek	152.9	9.8	11.1
Lawyer Hollow	154.0	10.9	10.0
National Forest Boundary	155.6	12.5	8.4
Leaning Rock Hollow	157.4	14.3	6.6
Park Service Boundary	159.4	16.3	4.6
The Narrows ('Nars)	162.8	19.7	1.2
Buffalo River (Woolum)	164.0	20.9	0.0

This section of trail is one of the most scenic and least used ones. There are lots of giant boulders, rock gardens, waterfalls and terrific views. The east end of this section* is difficult to get to — you either have to ford Richland Creek twice, or the Buffalo River once (or continue your hike downstream on the OHT/BRT Extension* to Tyler Bend or Hwy. 65 — see page 112). Another option is to get someone to ferry you across the Buffalo via canoe. *The BRT downstream from Woolum is now considered part of the OHT, although the original/classic end of the OHT is Woolum. Quad maps are Moore and Eula. GPS 35.79649° N, -92.93826°W

To get to Richland Creek Campground, take Hwy. 16 east from Pelsor (on Hwy. 7), about a mile past Ben Hur, then turn east onto FR# 1205 and follow it to the campground.

From Richland Creek Campground (143.1), the trail is on FR# 1205—TURN LEFT and follow the road down to the bridge across Richland Creek at 143.2. From the bridge continue on the road uphill a couple hundred feet. As the road turns sharp left, the trail takes off TO THE RIGHT into the

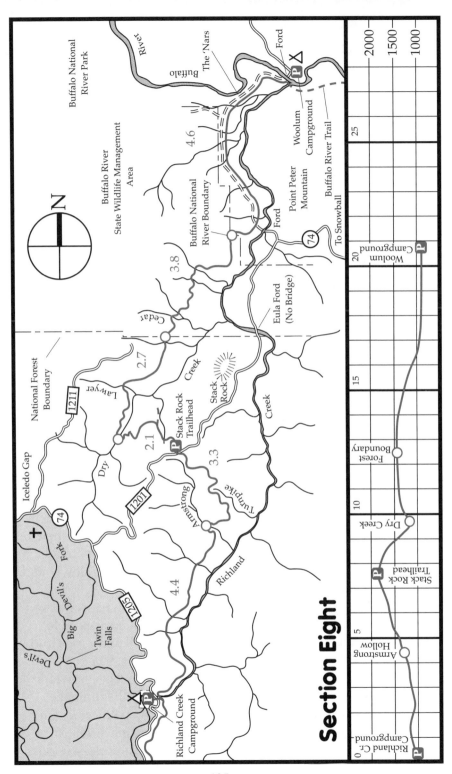

Section Eight

woods. It follows along a fairly level bench, just uphill from an old log road to the right.

During leaf–off you can look down onto Richland Creek and will have nice views up and down the valley. The trail continues along this bench for a while, working its way just slightly uphill. It runs across a more open wooded area, and past 144.0.

At 144.1 the trail intersects an old jeep road and TURNS LEFT and continues on this old road. Shortly afterward, a lesser road turns left — continue STRAIGHT AHEAD on the greater road. The terrain gets very steep here, and you can look straight down the hillside to the right onto Richland Creek. Nice views.

The trail remains level and on the road for a little while, passing a couple of giant boulders. Just beyond these boulders, the trail leaves the road TO THE RIGHT. It runs out into the woods, dropping slightly down onto a bench. It stays level on this bench for a while, then begins to climb just gradually, and a line of large boulders comes into view to the right.

The trail eases up the hill and turns back to the boulders, and then weaves its way through these moss–covered rocks, many larger than cars. From the boulder area, the trail continues on up and down a little, and passes 145.0.

From there the trail works its way into and across a neat little boulder–strewn creek. There are several of these creeks ahead, each with its own special magic, and lots of tumbling waterfalls during wet seasons.

This is a good place to caution you that in many areas for the next several miles you may encounter very rocky terrain. The footing is bad — there are either rocks sticking up everywhere or holes where rocks were removed. There is not really a "tread" in some areas — the trail is a little difficult to find so go slowly and be on the lookout for the trail corridor and blazes.

The trail continues on, and drops slightly down just below and past an area with lots of house–sized boulders (uphill to the left). Then it bumps up and over a small hill and drops into another rock–strewn paradise. This is Long Branch (145.4), an SSS. During wet seasons there are small waterfalls everywhere.

By 145.7 the trail has worked its way out of the drainage and is once again on a steep slope looking down onto Richland Creek. Wonderful views too, and the trail remains level. At 145.9 the trail goes up and around a large pile of loose rock — it looks man-made, but must be natural.

Before long the trail hits a jeep road and TURNS LEFT on the road. The road passes by a large boulder on the left, and just above it is another interesting giant boulder. At 146.5, the trail leaves this road TO THE RIGHT.

The trail continues on basically level, through lots of rocky areas with some up–and–downing. It crosses Drury Hollow at 146.8, another small boulder creek. Just beyond, there are some bluff formations uphill to the left. Further along on a level bench, the trail passes 147.0.

The trail stays on the level bench, then drops down into Armstrong Hollow, past some house–sized boulders. It crosses the creek at 147.5 on three tent–sized rocks. Another SSS area! Past the creek, there is some relief from the rocky road, as the trail goes through nice open woods, with some giant boulders scattered around here and there.

The trail crosses an old road, then remains level for a while, and at 148.2 it turns left and goes uphill. This is actually a switchback that takes you up to the next bench, and past some wonderful giant boulders — one of them with a sheltered spot to sit under. The whole area is an SSS.

Once on top, the trail turns back to the right, across almost level bench again. At 148.5 it intersects a four–wheeler trail and TURNS RIGHT. Several hundred feet later there is a trail that goes to the left — stay on the main trail for another hundred feet or so. Just as this begins to go downhill, the trail TURNS LEFT, and begins to climb. If you cross a creek here you've gone too far.

The trail follows a creek uphill, bends around to the left, and intersects a jeep road at 148.6. TURN RIGHT and continue uphill on this road. Turnpike Hollow Creek is visible to the right, and during wet seasons has some nice falls in it. As the road levels off there is a mound of dirt pushed up on it (to keep jeeps out — ha!). Just beyond this there is another jeep road that takes off back to the left — continue STRAIGHT AHEAD.

There is an interesting historical feature near the area of the dirt mound. Off in the woods to the right (across the creek) you will find a couple of unusual man-made rock features. These were used for storing "potato slips" way back when. I won't go into the whole story here, but if you ever run into an old timer from the area, ask about them.

At 148.8 the road makes a sharp turn to the right and crosses the creek. TURN LEFT at this intersection (don't cross creek), and continue up what looks like a lesser road, which soon turns to trail again. The trail continues on a slight uphill grade, comes alongside the creek, then crosses it. After a short climb, the trail levels off near 149.0.

Soon the trail crosses the jeep road that we had been on, then goes through some level forest with nice big trees in it. The trail crosses a small stream, climbs up, then switchbacks up to the left, runs level for a while, then turns back to the right again. It crosses a jeep road at 149.6, again at 149.7, and again at 149.8.

From this last jeep road, the trail stays level, just downhill of a road to the right, and passes 150.0. There are some nice views during leaf–off to the left. The trail stays basically level for a while, with only a slight uphill grade. It turns to the right and crosses a road at 150.4. It immediately crosses another road, then turns to the left and continues on the level, through some small thick timber. At 150.7 the trail crosses FR# 1201 (aka Richland Road)— this spot is three miles east of Dickey Junction.

The trail goes up a jeep road across the way to the Stack Rock OHT Trailhead (not to be confused with the Stack Rock Scenic Area Trailhead that is located .9 mile on down FR#1201 to the right). From the parking area the trail continues on the old road through a gate, dropping down the hill and back into the woods again. Soon the trail leaves the road TO THE LEFT.

The trail eases down and passes MILEPOST #151, then crosses a small creek. From the creek the trail swings around to the left a little and comes to a fork at 151.4—take the LEFT FORK.

The right fork is a blue-blazed side trail that drops through a small bluffline and heads .25 mile down past some giant boulders off to the left. When the side trail levels out there is an old homesite on the left with chimney, a couple of rotted logs and remains of a root cellar. Off to the right (bushwhack down) is Stack Rock Homestead Falls, which spills 35' over a ledge for a class D falls. This side trail was the original OHT, but had to be bypassed when a landslide took out a good part of the trail and hillside in 2017. OHTA volunteers built the reroute in 2018.

Back up on the main trail, it eases uphill just a little, then levels off and curves around to the left on a bench above a bluffline—some great SSS views during leaf-off of Horn

Mountain and distant Richland Valley—and more views as you work up into the Dry Creek Drainage past 152.0.

Watch out as the trail turns sharply right and drops down through a broken bluffline, swings right below the bluff and across a wide rocky bench, then left and downhill again, then rejoins the original OHT at 152.4 (you probably won't notice).

Soon the trail begins to switchback down the hill into the Dry Creek drainage. It crosses a jeep road, then soon after intersects with the same road for a 100 yards or so. TURN RIGHT off of this road, down to and across Dry Creek at 152.9. Across the creek the trail heads TO THE RIGHT (off road) up into the woods and climbs up a bench or two and passes 153.0. Some of this area is rough and rocky, but there are many nice views.

The trail eventually hits an old log road and TURNS RIGHT on it. Only for a couple hundred yards though, then it leaves the road to the RIGHT, and continues sort of on the level. It crosses several small drainages, then one that has some large rocks in it. This area begins an SSS, and is actually Lawyer Hollow, with several streams, and 154.0.

From this point on for a while the trail runs fairly level, past 155.0, and there are lots of nice views down into the Richland Creek Valley during leaf-off. You can also see a rock bluff area off in the distance that is known as "Stack Rock."

At 155.6 the trail leaves Ozark National Forest property and enters the Sutton Unit of the Buffalo Wildlife Management Area. It is owned by the Arkansas Game and Fish Commission. Don't be surprised if you see *elk* on this section. Or bears. One of the largest populations of bear in the state call this area home.

The trail is running along the east side of Horn Mountain, and if you are really energetic, up above the trail (several large benches up) is a tremendous bluff that runs for several miles.

At 155.8 the trail crosses a jeep road (go STRAIGHT) and becomes one itself. It drops down the hill a little and passes 156.0. Just beyond, the trail crosses a nice little stream, then curves up to the left through a real rocky area. It drops down to and across another small stream, then intersects an old road again — TURN LEFT and continue on the road. A couple hundred yards later the trail leaves the road (STRAIGHT AHEAD) into the woods.

At 156.5, there is a giant rock garden SSS. More level trail beyond, and at 156.75 there is also a house–sized boulder that just has to qualify as another SSS. The trail wraps right around it. Not too far beyond the trail bumps up over a slight rise and begins to drop down through a real rocky area. At 157.1 the trail splits two giant boulders — an SSS and a nice nap spot.

The trail exits the rocks to the left, remains level for a while, then drops down to and crosses Leaning Rock Hollow Creek at 157.4 — another SSS (bluffs uphill). It then heads downstream, then out across a wide, fairly level bench, and makes its way around the hill to 158.0. Soon the trail swings to the right, through an old rock wall, then intersects with a jeep road — TURN LEFT here and continue down the road.

This road winds around up and down, and at 158.7 intersects another old road — TURN LEFT. At 158.95 the road forks — take the RIGHT FORK. The road forks a couple more times — be sure to follow the blazes. At 159.4 the trail enters the boundary of the Buffalo National River. Stay on the road as it drops down the hill. It eventually comes out into an old grown–up homesite at 159.9, then intersects with a Park Service road. TURN LEFT on this road. You are now in the Richland Creek Valley, and the views are really nice. A hundred yards down this road is 160.0.

For the next four miles the trail is on this road (may not be blazes or mileposts). The route is easy to follow, and the only intersection is at 162.4 — stay to the RIGHT.

At 162.8 a large bluffline begins on the left, known as "The Narrows," and just on the other side is the Buffalo River (a trail leads up the bluff for a view). The road eventually comes out at the river at 164.0 and the original/historical end of the OHT. The Woolum access area is across the river (turn off of Hwy. 65 at Pendall or St. Joe to get there). *Caution: You may have to swim across the Buffalo River if ending here, which can be dangerous!*

The OHT continues east/downstream (as the OHT/BRT, or Buffalo River Extension of the OHT, all part of the Trans-Ozarks Trail)—turn the page for the map and hiking description!

SECTION NINE — 15.0 miles
Woolum to Grinders Ferry/Hwy. 65 Trailhead

Trail Point	Mile Point	Mileage West–East	Mileage East–West
Woolum	**164.0**	**0.0**	**15.0**
Point Peter Mountain	165.2	1.2	13.8
Ben Branch	167.5	3.5	11.5
Dave Manes Bluff	168.0	4.0	11.0
Hage Hollow Creek	170.1	6.1	8.9
Whisenant Hollow Bluffs	171.3	7.3	7.7
Tie Slide	173.2	9.2	5.8
Calf Creek	176.3	12.3	2.7
Collier Homestead TH	**177.1**	**13.1**	**1.9**
Tyler Bend VC (off trail)	178.5	(off trail) 14.5	(off trail) 1.3
Grinders Ferry TH/Hwy. 65	**179.0**	**15.0**	**0.0**

Section Nine of the OHT is the first of three OHT sections that have merged with the 43.6 mile lower stretch of the Buffalo River Trail (BRT). All are located within the Buffalo National River, which is America's first National River and was created in 1972. The park is administered by the National Park Service (headquarters are in Harrison, but the main visitor center is at Tyler Bend near the end of this section of trail).

You may see this beautiful stretch of trail labeled as the BRT Extension of the OHT, BRT/OHT, OHT/BRT, or simply OHT, but they are all the same trail—and are also part of the overall Trans-Ozarks Trail that will someday extend all the way to St. Louis.

Section Nine has some tremendous scenery, and because access to the upper end is limited it probably won't ever get a great deal of use. It begins in the Richland Creek Valley at the original terminus of the OHT (across the river from Woolum), runs across the tops of many bluffs that overlook the River, goes near Tyler Bend campground, then across Hwy. 65 to the Grinders Ferry Trailhead. It's blazed white (though not as many blazes as previous OHT sections), with yellow blazes for horse trails. **NOTE** that there currently are no physical mile posts along the trail, though we'll keep the mile points back to Lake Ft. Smith listed on the mileage logs. NO DOGS are allowed on the trail.

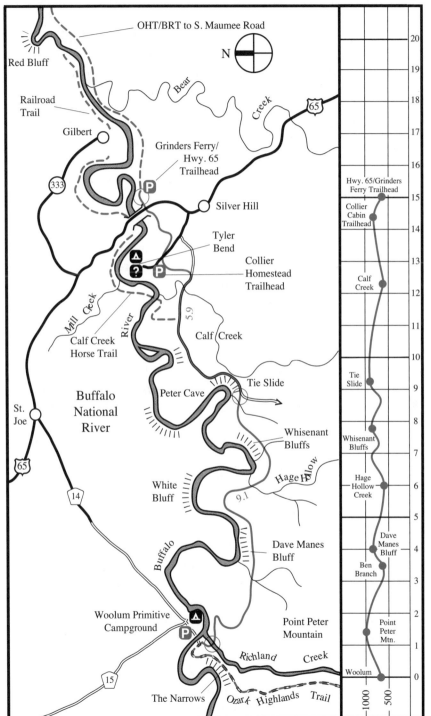

Getting to the beginning of this section can be a bit of a challenge. The easiest way is to go to the Woolum access on the River (turn off of Hwy. 65 at Pindall or St. Joe to get there). This area has primitive campsites and canoe access. Then you have to wade the Buffalo River. It is a wide crossing, that can be anywhere from knee-deep to over your head—and is **extremely dangerous to cross during high water**. Much of the time it is about waist deep, but it really depends on how high the River is running. If you are lucky, you can talk someone with a canoe there into running you across. If you wade the Buffalo, it is shallower to go across right where the road does, instead of trying it below Richland.

The only other way to get to the beginning of this section, is to drive in from the other end of the Richland Valley, on a dirt road. If you come in from Snowball, you'll have to ford Richland Creek once. If you come in from the Richland Creek Wilderness area, you'll have to ford Richland Creek twice. No problem either way, unless there is a lot of water in Richland!

A lot of this section of trail is on old roads, and there are a lot of intersections with other roads, as well as with the main horse trail in the area. It can get a little confusing at times. Be sure to keep an eye out for directional signs, and follow them.

So OK, here we go. This section begins just across the Buffalo from Woolum. The original/classic OHT ends here—if you continued on this road to the right you could hike 164 miles of trail, all the way to Lake Ft. Smith State Park on Hwy. 71. You want to go across Richland Creek. It is usually knee-deep or less, but often dry in the summer. Then cross the large field and head for the trail on the other side. This crossing is a couple hundred yards upstream from the mouth of Richland Creek.

The trail leaves the valley at .2, and heads *up* the hillside on some steps. It is pretty steep for a little while, and the trail switchbacks to the left. It eventually levels off somewhat, and you are looking right down on the River. The views, especially during leaf-off, are good. There is an SSS view at .5. Just beyond, the trail swings back to the right, away from the River. It works its way up and along the top of the ridge. This is part of Point Peter Mountain.

As the trail levels off on top at 1.0, there are several sinkholes next to the trail. Must be a cave around somewhere. It crosses a seep, and continues on the level, across the wide hilltop. At 1.2 there is an intersection. The trail/road to the right is a horse trail, and swings back down to Woolum. There are two trails/ roads to the left that you can take. The one on the left is level and again is a horse trail. The one on the right, which goes uphill just a little, is also a horse trail, but is not the one you want. So at the intersection, TURN LEFT and then TURN LEFT again (follow the sign).

The trail stays on the old road for a while, and pretty much just makes its way around Point Peter Mountain, staying up high. There are some good views along here during leaf-off, and an old homesite or two, plus an old car body, complete with tail fins. The trail runs along fairly level, with some up-and-downing. Then at about 2.7, it turns to the left, and begins a plunge down towards the River.

It does get steep at times—aren't you glad you're hiking it downhill! When you reach the bottom and level out, you come next to a nice little bluff-lined stream at 3.4. This is a minor SSS. You stroll along this pleasant creek, 'til you cross it at 3.5. This is Ben Branch.

Just around the corner there is an intersection. The main road heads uphill to the right. There is a lesser road that takes off to the left, down towards the River. There is also a path that goes STRAIGHT AHEAD and level—this is the one you want. After less than 100 feet, TURN RIGHT and you will be on good old plain American hiking trail. Yea! Old roads are a great way to get around these hills, but nothing beats properly constructed trail.

The trail heads up a small drainage, and gets a little steep as it swings back to the left. It levels off shortly, and from here on for a while it is just a wonderful hike. As it swings around to the right, there is a spur trail at 4.0, that leads a few feet out onto the edge of Dave Manes Bluff. This is the first of many SSS views that you have. The River sprawls out below you in both direc-tions (White Bluff looms above the River downstream). There are fields as far as you can see. And the immediate area around you has lots of craggy bluffs. It's time to drop your pack and take a break.

From the viewpoint, the trail continues along the top of the bluffline. There are lots of nice views. At 4.4 a road comes near the trail off to the right. There is an old field out there too. Just beyond, there is an unofficial spur trail to the left that leads out onto a "slice" of bluff—another SSS. The trail stays along the edge of the hillside for a little while longer, then swings back to the right, and leaves the River behind. It heads up a hollow, right next to a nice field on the right. It leaves this field, then comes alongside another, smaller one. At 4.8, just as the field ends, the trail intersects with a road—TURN LEFT on this road.

This begins another road section, but at least this part of the road is moss-covered. There is a lesser road that takes off to the right just ahead, but ignore it. At 5.1 there is a fork in the road— take the RIGHT HAND fork. It runs along on down the hillside to the bottom, where it comes out into a giant valley at 5.5, and another road. TURN RIGHT, and continue on the valley road. There is a wooden gate to the left, and an old car body to the right. At some point, you will be able to see some massive bluffs on downstream—these are located at Whisenant Hollow, and the trail runs on top of them at 7.3.

At 6.0 you need to TURN LEFT onto a road (the Slay family cemetery is hidden down a ways). Just down this road is where you will get back on "real" trail again—it takes off to the right. The trail crosses through the bottomland, across Hage Hollow Creek, then begins to work its way up a small hollow. It crosses this little stream several times. At 6.3 it joins an old, narrow, grown up road and heads steeply uphill. At 6.5 the trail leaves the road TO THE LEFT, and continues out through the woods, but still climbing.

It switchbacks a time or two, and finally, at 6.7 it swings over to the edge of the hillside, and overlooks the River at an SSS. It's a great view, and especially of those giant bluffs that are now much closer. The trail eases up the hill, levels off, then begins to descend. It lands at another SSS view, then continues *down* the hillside.

At 7.1, the trail crosses Whisenant Hollow, which is a small stream, then heads up the other side. It gets real steep as the trail switchbacks to the right, then to the left (if its real wet, you may hear and see a waterfall off in the woods). At 7.3 all is well again, as the trail has leveled off, and there is a spectacular view—you are now standing on those massive bluffs that you've been looking at.

And this is just the beginning. There are three SSS viewpoints right in a row. Each has a little different view of the bluffs and the world below. These bluffs are typical Buffalo River bluffs—a sheer face of solid limestone, painted with shades of gray and black and white, disappearing down into the forest below. Makes me wish I had wings.

The trail begins to drop off the hill a little, swings to the left, and then back to the right at 7.7. At this corner there is one last SSS view of the bluffs. From here the trail continues to drop down the hill, crosses a small creek, then runs up a short hill and turns to the right.

At 8.2 the trail goes across a dirt road and continues into the woods, veering off to the right some. A vast field comes into view off to the left, and the trail stays in the bottom for a while. There are a couple of unusual, eroded areas next to the trail. At 8.7 the trail TURNS RIGHT up a gravel creek bottom, then leaves the creek and heads up the hill to the left.

It climbs up the hillside, swings back to the left, then back to the right. The last part gets steep, but during leaf-off a view opens up to help you manage the stress. The trail runs along the top of the ridge, veers away from it for a little while, then back to it. The trail runs just on the left side of the hill, and the views keep getting better.

At 9.2 is an SSS view that it is a historical spot too—the "Tie Slide." Way back when, as the mighty white oak trees in this area were being cut down to be made into railroad ties, this spot was used to "slide" the logs, down along a cable, to the gravel bar below. It must have been an impressive sight, but I sure do like the way things look now. If you need to take a break, wait just a few more minutes.

Right past the Tie Slide, the trail hits a road—TURN LEFT on this road. You will be on this road all the way to the Tyler Bend area. The road swings to the right, away from the River for a short distance, then rejoins the edge of the hillside. And at 9.7, there is a cleared trail spur off to the left—this is where you need to stop and take a break—for it is a terrific SSS area!

In my humble opinion, this is one of the ten best views on the River. Craggy bluffs, twisted cedars, the River and valley below stretching out forever. Yea, its an SSS alright. A place I plan to return many times. And down below, somewhere among the crags, is Peter Cave (may be gated/closed). Enjoy this view, 'cause there aren't many more views of the River for a while.

From here the trail remains on the road, and runs along level. During leaf-off, you may be able to look out to the right and see the Calf Creek drainage. You'll be crossing Calf Creek in a few miles. At 10.3 the road forks. The left fork will take you down towards Cash Bend on the River. You want to take the RIGHT FORK for the main trail. There are several lesser roads that intersect with the one you are on— stay on the main road.

By 11.3, the trail hits bottom and begins a long, level walk through several grown-up farmsteads. There is a pond on the right. In the late and early spring the honeysuckle perfume makes this a very pleasant hike. There is a hill and bluff off to the left that come into view—you'll be climbing up that hill shortly. The bluff is up on the River View Trail at Tyler Bend.

You'll pass the remains of the Arnold house at 12.0. Then Calf Creek appears below the road on the left. You get a good look at the hillside you're about to climb up to. At 12.3 you cross Calf Creek. This is a wide, gravel-bottomed crossing, that is usually about mid-calf deep (but can get much deeper).

Past the creek, the road winds through a wonderful field. This was the last section of trail that I did for the first edition of this guide. It was late in the day, in mid-May when I did it. The sun was low and golden. The field was full of purple flowers, and bright green hay, and the air was alive with a hundred of those small butterflies. It had been a long day, indeed a long several months of gathering information for this book. And I think that the field knew that my hiking was coming to an end (for now). It wanted to bid a fond farewell, and this pastoral scene was just the trick. I just had to pause, and soak up all the beauty, one more time.

But you're not finished hiking yet, so lets continue through to the end of the field. Just as the road enters woods again at 12.5, the trail, and I do mean just trail, TURNS LEFT, and heads up the hillside into the woods. It climbs on *up*, and there is one great view of the Calf Creek Valley. At 13.0 it comes to the Collier Homestead, and connects with the River View Trail, which goes 1.5 miles to the Tyler Bend Visitor Center. To continue with the Buffalo River Trail, TURN RIGHT.

The trail goes over to the Collier Homestead Trailhead (this part is wheelchair accessible) at 13.1. You are now in the Tyler Bend Recreation Area (see detail map opposite page). There are four short trails in the park, and all of them connect to the OHT/ BRT. (And dogs are allowed on these short trails as of 2021!)

From the trailhead, the OHT/BRT crosses the paved entrance

road to the park, and continues out into the woods. It intersects with the Spring Hollow Trail at 13.5 (turn left for it). The main trail GOES STRAIGHT. It gradually climbs up to and around the head of a hollow, and comes to the Buck Ridge Trail at 14.1 (turn left for it). The main trail TURNS RIGHT and heads across the head of another hollow.

At 14.6 it comes to the Rock Wall Trail (again, turn left for it). The main trail GOES STRAIGHT, and heads down the hillside towards Hwy. 65. Before it gets there, it makes its way down the hill some, passes under a powerline, then drops down to and across a small stream twice, and finally comes out at the end of the Hwy. 65 bridge over the Buffalo. The main OHT/BRT continues through a giant culvert under Hwy. 65 (if frozen BE CAREFUL!!!—perhaps detour up to the highway and down the other side). From the culvert the trail runs mostly level out to and across the Grinders Ferry access road and Trailhead, ending this section of the trail at 15.0.

Tyler Bend Trails

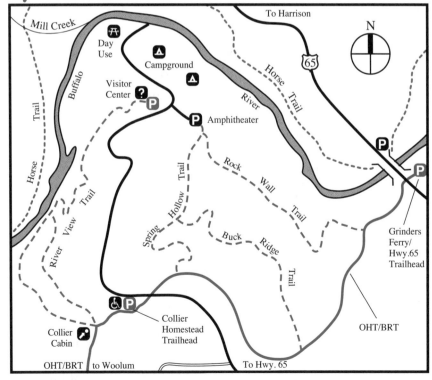

SECTION TEN — 17.3 miles
Grinders Ferry/Hwy. 65 Trailhead to South Maumee Road

Trail Point	Mile Point	Mileage West–East	Mileage East–West
Grinders Ferry TH/Hwy. 65	**179.0**	**0.0**	**17.3**
Long Bottom Road	180.6	1.6	15.7
Illinois Point	180.9	1.9	15.4
Amphitheater Falls	181.7	2.7	14.6
Gilbert Overlook	183.1	4.1	13.2
Bear Creek	184.8	5.8	11.5
Zack Ridge Road TH	**185.6**	**6.6**	**10.7**
Brush Creek	186.7	7.7	9.6
Red Bluff Spur Trail	187.5	8.5	8.8
Red Bluff Road TH	**190.1**	**11.1**	**6.2**
Rocky Creek	192.0	13.0	4.3
Little Rocky Creek	193.3	14.3	3.0
Pileated Point	193.5	14.5	2.8
Hoot-Owl Hollow	194.7	15.7	1.6
Saw-Whet Owl Falls	195.0	16.0	1.3
South Maumee Road TH	**196.3**	**17.3**	**0.0**

This is a continuation of the OHT/BRT from the Grinders Ferry Trailhead (Hwy. 65) to the South Maumee Road Trailhead (the final stretch was completed in 2021). There are lots of amazing views, several nice waterfalls, and a few steep climbs that will make ya wish you'd cut that toothbrush in half! There are also a couple of large creeks to cross that could be **dangerous during high water** (Bear Creek and Brush Creek) so plan accordingly. Blazed white, NO DOGS.

The trailhead is located just off of Hwy. 65 between Marshall and St. Joe (and just down the road from the Tyler Bend area). Grinders Ferry is also one of the major canoe access points on the River so you'll find a lot of traffic there. GPS 35.98420, -92.74422

The trail leaves the parking lot to the RIGHT of the rest rooms, heads up a short spur trail that leads to the main trail, then TURNS LEFT onto the OHT/BRT. It heads off mostly level through the woods and passes a small food plot on the left. It keeps going straight, and then at .1 we merge with an old road that comes down from the right. We just continue

OHT/BRT Section Ten (Grinders Ferry to S. Maumee Rd)

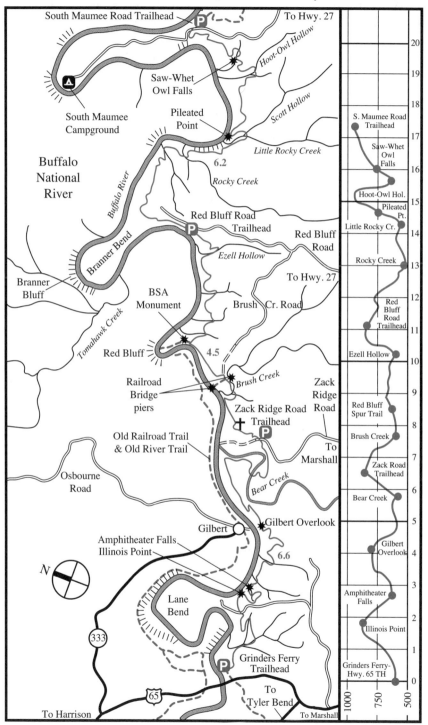

South Maumee Road Trailhead

To Hwy. 27

Hoot-Owl Hollow

Saw-Whet
Owl Falls

Scott Hollow

South Maumee
Campground

Pileated
Point

Little Rocky Creek

6.2

Buffalo
National
River

Rocky Creek

Buffalo River

Red Bluff Road
Trailhead

Red Bluff
Road

Branner Bend

Ezell Hollow

To Hwy. 27

Branner
Bluff

BSA
Monument

Brush Cr. Road

Tomahawk Creek

Red Bluff

4.5

Railroad
Bridge
piers

Brush Creek

Zack
Ridge
Road

Zack Ridge Road
Trailhead

Old Railroad Trail
& Old River Trail

To
Marshall

Osbourne
Road

Bear Creek

Gilbert Overlook

Gilbert

Amphitheater Falls
Illinois Point

6.6

N

Lane
Bend

333

Grinders Ferry
Trailhead

65

To
Tyler Bend

To Harrison

To Marshall

S. Maumee Road
Trailhead

Saw-Whet
Owl
Falls

Hoot-Owl Hol.

Pileated
Pt.

Little Rocky Cr.

Rocky Creek

Red
Bluff
Road
Trailhead

Ezell Hollow

Red Bluff
Spur Trail

Brush Creek

Zack Road
Trailhead

Bear Creek

Gilbert
Overlook

Amphitheater
Falls

Illinois Point

Grinders Ferry-
Hwy. 65 TH

20
19
18
17
16
15
14
13
12
11
10
9
8
7
6
5
4
3
2
1
0

1000 750 500

straight ahead, easing down the hill along the road next to the food plot/old field.

The old roadbed swings around to the right just a little bit, and at .3 down on the left is the foundation of the Grinder's home site (the folks who operated the ferry in the 1800's). From there the trail is still on the road and continues to curve back to the right and begins to work itself downhill slightly and up into a side drainage. Pretty soon the trail levels, passes a small pond on the left and then continues on over to and across a creek at .4.

The trail follows the little creek up into Goodhue Hollow, crossing small forks of it a couple of times as it works up into this side drainage. By .8 the trail is easing up the hill a little more aggressively, above the creek that's down on the left. At 1.0 we turn to the LEFT and switchback across the creek.

From the creek crossing, the trail eases uphill and swings to the right towards the top of the ridge, passing through a thick grove of cedar trees, and leaf-off views begin to open up a bit. We continue across the ridge to the right and then back to the left, straighten out, and cross Long Bottom Road at 1.6. (This road goes to the left down to Lane Bend, and to the right back out to Hwy. 65 at Silver Hill.)

The trail continues on the other side of the road and levels out along the left side of a ridge. During leaf-off you get some real nice views back to the left towards Lane Bend, and also out to both Pilot and Boat mountains in the distance. It's really steep below you, looking straight down towards the River—this stretch is kind of a moving SSS. And then we come out to Illinois Point overlook at 1.9, a great SSS looking both up and downstream and across towards the community of Gilbert. (A group of volunteers from Illinois built much of this section of trail, hence the name.)

From the overlook, the trail switchbacks to the RIGHT and begins a descent across the steep hillside down into a hollow. At 2.0 the trail levels off and swings to the left around the head of this small drainage above one of the small prongs (usually dry). It crosses a small road and continues over to the edge of a major powerline right-of-way at 2.3 (you can look all the way down to the River). The trail switchbacks TO THE LEFT just before you enter the opening and heads back into the hollow you just left.

The trail drops down the hill and works its way back into the hollow (across the little road again), and at 2.4 it crosses the hollow in two spots. If there is a lot of water flowing then you're in for a nice treat at the bottom of the hill. The trail swings back to the right and continues to cut across very steep hillside working its way quickly downhill above the little creek below to the right. The trail gets a little closer to the creek and at 2.5 down to the right is the top of a waterfall. It's extremely dangerous there, so stay away from the top—the trail will take you to the bottom in a few moments for a much safer view!

The trail continues down and comes to the edge of that same powerline. TURN RIGHT and head downhill and curve around away from the powerline and soon you will arrive near the bottom of the waterfall at 2.7, which is located just over a little gravel hump on the right. This is Amphitheater Falls, 47', a major SSS. Hum, time for a snack break.

From the bottom of the waterfall, the trail swings away to the LEFT and follows the creek downstream (you'll be in the creek or just up on the right hillside—the trail may be sketchy through here), then back to the powerline, which may be pretty grown up. Go across the powerline and at the end of the right-of-way the trail leaves the creek to the RIGHT on good trail and heads upstream on another side creek—Boone Hollow. Follow this until it crosses the creek at 2.8 at a little limestone slide. There's a nice little waterfall and you cross just above that.

On the other side, the trail curves back to the left, mostly on the level and follows the creek downstream towards the Buffalo River. The trail swings to the right and goes across a steep hillside. The trail drops down the hill just a little into the bottom near the River on a little bit of a bench to 3.0. At this point you are just upstream from Gilbert.

At 3.1 we bump up the hill just a little to a small bluff on the right, then the trail switchbacks to the RIGHT just below that bluff and heads up a side drainage and away from the River, slightly uphill. Soon the trail crosses that creek, switchbacks to the left, and begins one of the more difficult climbs in this first section.

Switchback to the right. Switchback to the left. Switchback to the right. Continue pretty steep. Switchback to the left, continue up but not quite as steep. In fact, it kind of levels off a bit and goes around the nose of the ridge where you can see Gilbert, also it's straight down to the River. At 3.5, still up on the hillside and mostly level, we turn away from the River and work up into another drainage.

By 3.7, the trail has worked its way downhill just slightly to and across a little creek and there's a neat little stair-step waterfall there. And then the trail switchbacks to the left going back uphill, though not nearly as steep as the last drainage. We come up to the nose of a ridge, curve around to the right, slightly uphill. At that curve you have another good look across at Gilbert. Then we work our way back to the head of a little hollow and level off at 4.0.

The trail continues, actually easing on down the hill just a little bit across a steep hillside. Then we come out to the nose of another ridge and curve around it. It's a pretty good view from up there, especially during leaf-off—Gilbert Overlook. At 4.3 we're continuing mostly level across a very steep hillside, dropping down the hill a little bit. Pretty nice, easy trail, good views.

At 4.5 we intersect an old road and we continue going STRAIGHT down the hill on the roadbed. It gets pretty steep going downhill. But just a couple a hundred feet down, the road intersects with another one. TURN LEFT on this old road heading downhill. There's yucca plants on either side of the turn.

At 4.6 the road makes a sharp switchback to the RIGHT and down the hill. The old road bed that goes straight ahead is where the old River crossing via ferry was, but we want to switchback to the RIGHT. The Buffalo River is kind of right in front of us and down below, and we're headed back downstream. Quickly the road levels off, and we stay on this roadbed in the bottom straight and level.

At 4.9 there's a historical landmark in the middle of the trail/ road—an old washing machine tub! Just beyond the tub we head uphill on the old road bed. At 5.0 we're still on the roadbed. It's kind of easing up. Continue on the road, slightly uphill, then it levels off.

The Buffalo River has been off on our left, out through the trees, but soon the trail/road gets rocky, and we turn away from the River to the right, and begin to head downhill just a little bit, eventually leaving the old road behind. We begin to work our way up the Bear Creek drainage, and come alongside this beautiful stream at 5.3. Some nice big boulders along the edge. SSS!

We continue along the bank of Bear Creek on the level sandy trail through a thick stand of river cane. At 5.5 the trail veers to the RIGHT away from the creek and cuts across the flat and into the woods. It eases uphill a little bit, goes up and over a little rise, then starts to drop down back to the creek next to a small bluff line on the right, soon leveling off back next to Bear Creek. At 5.8 we come to and cross Bear Creek on a diagonal.

Most of the year this a wet crossing, so plan to wade. In the summer you might be able to find a spot to cross dry but it's pretty wide. During high-water events this would be extremely dangerous and you are best to turn back, especially if you can't see the bottom of the creek.

Once across the creek follow the trail on up over to the edge of a pasture, where the trail turns LEFT and goes around the pasture. The trail curves around to the right off the end of the pasture, then starts to head up the hill, leaving the pasture behind.

The trail crosses a small creek then continues through the woods uphill and to the right, then up against a fence (private property) at 6.1, where it curves to the LEFT. It continues up and around and past the fence, crossing a very steep hillside during a sustained climb. As the trail climbs it's a great SSS view during leaf-off looking out over Bear Creek and beyond. If you get off the trail here you might roll all the way down to the creek, so be careful!

At 6.4 the trail levels out for a moment at a switchback, and there's a blue-blazed side trail that goes to the left and downhill a bit to a wonderful SSS overlook of the Bear Creek Valley called Crane Bottom, and beyond. The main trail cuts back up the hill to the RIGHT, and climbs steadily until it reaches the Zack Ridge Road and Trailhead at 6.6.

To get to this trailhead from Harps on Hwy. 65 in Marshall—head north on Zack Ridge Road and go 7.0 miles to the trailhead on the right (paved, then dirt). GPS 35.99087, -92.69601. *Currently the trailhead is only a wide spot in the road with limited parking, but there will be a real trailhead here soon we hope.

Once across the road, the trail heads back into the woods on the LEFT, and runs mostly level and passes through a cedar thicket to the right. There's a pond just beyond and the trail goes to the far end of the pond and turns left and follows along the top of the pond, then leaves the pond bank to the right and back down into the cedar thicket again—kind of a neat little swing around the pond.

You'll notice some old piles of rock along the trail for a while—sometimes farmers piled rocks while clearing fields instead of building rock walls. The trail drops on down to a second pond at 6.85, and it follows along the pond bank again, heading off into the woods on the other end still following those rock piles (when used for direction they would be called cairns).

We ease up a hill just a little bit, and at 6.9 we curve around to the RIGHT and actually go around Horton Cemetery, a tiny pioneer cemetery with only a few headstones left.

From the cemetery the trail continues straight and actually begins to ease down the hill past 7.0, levels off a bit then a gentle grade. You veer over to the edge and see the Buffalo River directly below, and a real nice SSS view looking upstream. In fact SSS views for a while, up and downstream.

At 7.3 you can see historic concrete railroad trestle piers just downstream. The M&NA—Missouri and North Arkansas Railroad, AKA "May Never Arrive"—was built and ran in the early 1900's, and was dismantled in 1949, leaving the towering piers behind. They're about 35 feet tall and were totally submerged during a big flood in 1982.

The trail at that point curves around to the RIGHT and begins to work its way into a side drainage and away from the River. It drops through a rocky little bluffy area and then it switchbacks back and forth to the bottom and at 7.6 we come to and cross the creek, with a small waterfall there. Once across the creek, the trail turns to the LEFT and follows the creek downstream.

From that point we intersect with a road, an old overgrown road coming in from the right. We just keep going straight ahead, passing the remains of a little old rock shelter. Just beyond the shelter we come to Brush Creek at 7.7. This is a pretty big creek crossing and obviously dangerous during high water! The trail crosses on an angle upstream to the RIGHT (should be a white blaze on a tree).

Once across the creek head RIGHT/upstream until you intersect with a jeep road. Go LEFT on that road, which goes up the little hill (don't turn right and cross the creek again). This is Brush Creek Road, and it gets kinda washed out and rough, curves back around to the right, then levels off.

At 7.8 if you look below you to the right there's a short pair of concrete piers, one on either side of Brush Creek, where there used to be a trestle for the railroad. And on the left is the old railroad bed that's marked with blue blazes—this is a spur trail that goes about a quarter mile over to a set of those much taller and impressive piers standing tall in the Buffalo River. Worth a side trip and maybe lunch!

The main trail/road tops out at 7.9 and the trail leaves the road to the LEFT. Go straight along a line of cedar trees on the level, then soon the trail veers away from the cedars to the right, and joins another old road bed, then intersects with a jeep road. TURN LEFT onto that road and follow it downhill past 8.0.

The River is out there a couple of hundred yards through the woods and we're hiking mostly level and straight. Just as we're getting a little closer to the River at 8.3, the road swings to the left towards the River, but trail continues STRAIGHT AHEAD as plain trail, on the level. (A horse trail marked with yellow blazes shares the same route for a while.)

The trail goes up through a small bluffy area and on top of a small bluff. As we climb up here there's a bigger bluff above us to the right. We level off a little bit. Nice views looking down to the River to a big gravel bar.

At 8.5 we come to a trail intersection. A blue-blazed spur trail goes to the left to a Boy Scout monument built in 1972, and that's also the horse trail. That side trail also goes about a half mile over to the Buffalo River near the base of Red Bluff (great gravel bar for camping).

Back on the OHT/BRT, it TURNS RIGHT at the intersection and goes back through a neat little rock wall, then we curve around to the left past it on the level. The trail winds around a bit through an old homesite area and along an old road trace in parts, rocky in places.

At 8.8, we come to and across a creek with a small SSS waterfall. Then the trail follows along beside what I call a wave bluff. It's only 10 or 12 feet tall and it's like a wave frozen in time looming over you. The trail continues along an ancient road bed, eases up the hill, crosses a glade area with a cactus or two, and lots of ferns with rich and lush but shallow dirt.

We continue up this old road trace out of the glade area into the woods past 9.0, then leaving the road we swing to the LEFT and cross a little drainage. The trail eases on up the hill through the woods, a little steeper now winding through moss covered boulder fields. It swings around to the left, and levels out a bit.

At 9.2 as the trail is crossing a steep hillside around the nose of the ridge, there's an SSS view down to the River, especially looking downstream. Real nice spot. The trail eases across that steep hillside and SSS views continue.

The trail begins to ease on down the hill a bit into Wolf Hollow, and then down at a pretty good clip. We're at 9.4 and we are heading away from the River into this hollow so we've lost our great view. We come down to the bottom and creek at 9.5 and we turn LEFT. The trail follows an old roadbed for a little bit, and eventually heads uphill away from the creek.

It continues uphill on trail only through rocky hillside, and lots of mossy rocks and ledges. Levels off for a little bit. During leaf-off there are more nice views down the River. At 9.7 the trail makes a run up the hill along the face of another really steep hillside and beautiful SSS view during leaf-off, with the River right below us. Levels off through more rocks and great views downstream and upstream, then we start to ease on down the hill across the same steep hillside. The trail curves around to the left, away from the River. It goes to a little rocky area, makes a switchback to the left and then to the right, switchbacking down through a moss-covered rocky area and then straightens out.

From there the trail eases on downhill a little bit, winds around through a rocky stretch and comes to 10.0. By the way, we're back away from the River here in a little hollow. At 10.1 we continue to drop downhill and go through a small bluffy area. We're getting down close to River level, but we're in heavy woods away from it, then hike on the level through canebrake. Most of the time when you walk through canebrake like this you know the River's not too far away, although sometimes the longest way to get there is to go straight through the canebrake.

As you are roaming along the bottom, the trail swings to the right beneath and through some nice big trees over next to a creek, Ezell Hollow, crossing it at 10.2. You cross it on a diagonal and then follow the creek upstream just gradually going uphill. Get ready for one of the steepest climbs in this section where the trail has to climb to avoid private property.

The trail continues uphill, up into the drainage, climbing away from the creek. We're at 10.3 now. Still climbing. The trail at 10.4 continues uphill, kind of steep, crossing pretty steep, rocky hillside. Then we come up against a small bluff and the trail switchbacks to the left and goes up a series of ledges. Straight up. And then it curves to the right and levels off for a moment, then continues up through this ledge-rock steep hillside, heading upstream away from the Buffalo.

The trail switchbacks to the left in the middle of the steep part, continues up a couple of more quick ziggy zaggy, straight up the hill, left and right. More ziggy zaggy up through 10.5. It keeps going up. Finally the trail straightens out a little bit, still uphill, and this time headed back towards the Buffalo River. The worst part is over.

At 10.6 we pass a property corner on the right. We're still headed uphill through the woods, parallel to the River, but out of sight. At 10.7 we level off on that steep hillside, come up to a small bluff on the right, and a good leaf-off view down to the River into the hills beyond. The trail brushes against the bluff and then eases uphill a little bit. SSS views in this area both upstream and downstream.

The trail runs level again, then slightly downhill across the same steep hillside with great views downstream and of the big pasture across the way. By 11.0 it has leveled out and looking downstream you can see Branner Bend in the River ahead. The trail runs slightly up the hill to an intersection with a spur trail at 11.1—up to the RIGHT is the Red Bluff Road Trailhead.

To get to the trailhead from Marshall—go north on Hwy. 27 for 4.0 miles then TURN LEFT onto paved Trout Farm Road (Howard Hensley WMA sign), go 3.0 miles and TURN RIGHT onto Red Bluff Road (gravel), then go 2.3 miles and TURN RIGHT onto Red Bluff Road/CR#49, go 1.5 miles to the trailhead on the left. GPS 36.01624, -92.65714. Currently the trailhead is only a wide spot in the road with limited parking, but there will be a real trailhead here soon, we hope.

BACK out on the OHT/BRT, the main trail TURNS RIGHT and continues level along a very steep hillside that gets thick with old twisted cedars. A hundred yards from the trailhead is a nice cut-out SSS view looking down to the River, pastures and hills behind, with Pilot Mountain in the distance. Beautiful!

You'll also see the upstream side of an acute bend in the River just ahead, Branner Bend, and the 170 foot tall Branner Bluff at the far end of that bend across the River. Both were named after John C. Branner, Arkansas State Geologist, 1887–1893. Dr. Branner led a team that included future US President Herbert Hoover (then a student at Stanford) that documented prominent geological features in this area, including several major fault lines that cross the Buffalo River and OHT/BRT (Tomahawk Fault and North Rocky Creek Fault). Dr. Branner's accomplishments while in Arkansas have been largely ignored in the history books but he certainly deserves credit for moving our geological history and facts giant steps forward. Interestingly, he was kind of run out of the state in 1893 after he exposed a $100+ million dollar scheme by gold prospecting companies after he announced that there was no gold in the Ouachita mountains. He moved on to become the President of Stanford University. And now we have Branner Bluff and Branner Bend to rekindle some of that history.

One other note about the Branner Bend area—it was one of the first known bald eagle nesting sites along the Buffalo River in modern times, discovered by Jim Liles (Liles Falls is named after him), and his bride, Suzy. Jim designed and built a lot of this section of the trail to South Maumee Road. (Jim was the former Assistant Superintendent at Buffalo National River, and Suzy the former historian.)

Beyond the scenic overlook, the trail is still on the level, then it curves to the right away from the River, so you just lost your view. It cuts across a steep hillside then slightly downhill, passing under a powerline.

The trail continues and crosses an old roadbed, then drops down to and across a road at 11.4. This old road goes down near the River and is closed to public vehicle use, but open to hiking so it might be a great side trip to the River (hum, and maybe a great gravel bar campsite?). So just keep going straight across the road into the woods slightly downhill. The trail wraps around a hill to the right, across the face of a ridge and another old road trace, and works its way slightly downhill away from the River and into a hollow.

At 11.7 the trail comes to a wet area with huge ferns (glade ferns and Christmas ferns depending on time of year). During wet weather there's a waterfall on the right branch and one on the main branch. You cross the creek there. It's very lush and tropical and I'd say a nice little SSS area.

The trail crosses another old road trace and continues along the same hillside, easing up at a steady pace. Trail is on a steady grade up the hillside. At 12.0 we're in the middle of that climb, then eventually the trail tops out and levels off on top of a small double-deck bluff. Kind of a neat spot during leaf-off, an SSS area. Time to slow down, look around, nice view upstream, lots of moss and stuff, and a gigantic cedar tree.

At 12.3 the trail switchbacks to the LEFT down off the bluff and down through it. It's just a short switchback left a couple of steps, and then switchback right, continuing down in between bluff lines. Then it levels out for just a minute below one of the little bluff lines. Along the lower bluff line you can see some calcite formations dripping underneath it. It's actual calcium carbonate clay formations, little stalactites on the wall. But just past that little bluff, the trail switchbacks sharply to the LEFT and downhill. As we head on down the hillside it switchbacks to the right again, almost onto itself, continues down the hill, winding down through rocks and small bluffs and nice big trees.

Then we get down below the bluffs and it levels off a bit and straightens out through thick brush. A little ways beyond 12.5 the trail switchbacks to the left, continues downhill a little bit, then runs level. At 12.6 it turns to the right and drops down to and across a creek.

From the creek we head uphill on an old road bed, then turn to the LEFT onto a jeep road of sorts. We're on that road for a hundred feet and then we turn to the RIGHT, leave the road and we're on plain trail going through heavy canebrake. We know the River is nearby when we see all this river cane, and then shortly the trail turns to the RIGHT away from the cane and eases uphill just a little bit.

This trail just eases uphill and, oh my goodness, it is a jungle! Thick vines. It takes a lot of volunteer maintenance to keep this corridor open—you've got to thank the volunteers! (and perhaps adopt a section of this trail to maintain) It takes lots of cutting back every year to keep the corridor open for hiking. The trail levels off, swings to the left on an old road trace and then the trail leaves it to the LEFT and drops down in the woods at 12.8.

We get down near the bottom of the hill and land on a little roadbed that runs near Rocky Creek, then soon makes a sharp LEFT off of the old roadbed. That takes us over into a level open area right next to the creek—head out across the middle of this area going upstream (look for white blazes). There are some really big sycamore trees. As the valley begins to narrow, the trail turns LEFT and crosses Rocky Creek at 13.0.

Once across the creek the trail turns to the RIGHT and goes underneath one of the world's largest grapevines! Just past the grapevine it switchbacks to the LEFT and climbs up the hill back in the direction of the Buffalo. At 13.2 we swing around up through a little point of a ridge with small bluffs and there's a set of Buffalo River rapid's right below us. Good place to stop for a minute to take in the beauty.

From there, the trail curves back to the RIGHT and continues uphill away from the River. More uphill and we swing to the left. And then at 13.6 we hit a Jeep road. TURN RIGHT onto that Jeep road. Watch for this turn if coming from the other direction. The jeep road runs level, then starts to head STEEPLY up the hill for another tough climb.

The road turns back to the left (there's a big old slab of rock holding up the tree up on the right), and then it switchbacks to the right as it climbs up the hill. Switchback to the left, go up steep again. Then at 13.5, as the road switchbacks to the right again, the trail leaves the road to the LEFT on the level, you can celebrate here, and continues into the woods as plain trail. Whew, good job!

As you head out on this level trail across a steep hillside you'll have nice leaf-off views looking downstream and to the River. This stretch for a while is all an SSS. Very nice trail. But be CAREFUL—the trail runs along the top of a bluff close to the edge, and if you do happen to fall in this section, lean *into* the hillside. (Just sayin'!)

Soon the trail heads downhill and works its way up into a drainage away from the Buffalo. At 13.8 we intersect with a logging road. We turn LEFT and follow the logging road downhill. Soon there's an intersection and the road turns sharply to the RIGHT and we switchback downhill to the right, then go swiftly downhill now into a small hollow on a rough old roadbed to 13.9 (this used to be Grandview Road).

The trail leaves the roadbed TO THE RIGHT and continues as normal trail across a rocky hillside. It crosses a small stream then rises up to the base of a bluff, zigzags up, levels out for a moment, then zigzags back down through the broken bluff. The trail runs to the right, over to a step down through a smaller bluff, then switchbacks steeply down to a flight of stone steps into a beautiful/narrow creek. Upstream is an SSS waterfall that's quite delightful during high water. Another flight of stone steps takes you out of the creek, across a flat and rejoins the old roadbed at 14.0—TURN RIGHT and follow the old roadbed.

The trail is running upstream alongside Little Rocky Creek and crosses the main fork that comes in from the right at 14.3. Continue to the LEFT across a second fork, which is Scott Hollow— a nice little hole of water there—all of this is a nice SSS. Go STRAIGHT across, and the trail continues on the other side.

From the creek, the trail goes up in the woods and turns to the LEFT, and starts easing up the hill, going back downstream towards the Buffalo River. The trail climbs steadily till 14.5. Just as you're about to come out on a point, it switchbacks to the RIGHT and continues uphill. (If you go **off-trail straight ahead** at that switchback there's a spectacular SSS view of the River upstream and downstream, called Pileated Point. Maybe you can spot or hear the giant bird that was the inspiration for Walt Disney's famous Woody Woodpecker character.)

Back on the main trail however we are headed for another pretty tough climb up a very steep hillside that is just kind of rocks, small bluffs, and more rocks. The trail zigzags up and up and up. No need to hurry—the hill will wait on you to catch our breath. By 14.7 it is still uphill but you leave the worst of the rocky area and climbing behind.

At 14.9 we come to the end of the climb and to a saddle where the trail intersects an old road, which is a great place to stop and breathe after that climb! (At this intersection there is an old road back to the left that makes a loop around the hill—I'm told this was where log trucks used to be able to use the loop around the hill to turn around.)

From the trail intersection in the saddle, TURN RIGHT and head uphill on an old road. You can't really tell it's much of a road, just following the center of the narrow ridge. A little bit of view to the left during leaf-off, looking downstream. If your car is parked at the South Maumee Trailhead, that's where it's going to be—up on top of that far away ridge over there.

Near the top of that saddle at 15.0 the trail veers to the LEFT. You don't really notice that you've left the road, but you have. And you join another little road that you will follow going down-hill. As we continue down this logging road at a pretty good clip you can look out during leaf-off and see the River on the left. Pretty nice view. At 15.3 the trail leaves the old road bed to the LEFT and cuts below the road bed heading downhill.

The trail drops on down past a set of short bluffs, then comes to a neat big block of stone that is sitting on the left at 15.4 (Ken Smith calls it Dog's Head Rock). Please don't push it over!

Then the trail levels off and continues above the bluff—be careful where you step and don't go over the edge. At 15.5 you cross a slippery little creek on the steep hillside, and just past a couple of boulders the trail takes a HARD LEFT and it goes straight DOWN the hill. Potentially a very slick area - be careful.

Pick your way down the hill, then the trail veers over to the RIGHT and becomes actual trail again. The trail levels off at a moss covered rock slide that's a beautiful SSS. This area is called Christmas Hollow, and when the water's flowing well look above to see Christmas Hollow Falls, a beautiful SSS!

Once across the creek, the trail continues heading downstream and then levels off and swings over to the RIGHT and heads up into Hoot-Owl Hollow. Small hollows like this dry up quickly in the summer, although I was saved one hot August afternoon when I arrived with no water (having started the day at Grinders Ferry)—crystal clear magical stuff bubbled out of the ground from a tiny spring in the creek—I sat on the ground and drank a full liter of cold spring water! (filtered of course)

Soon the trail swings to the LEFT and crosses the creek at 15.7. From the creek the trail heads uphill and just about a hundred feet up the hill it goes past a pit dug by a mineral prospector. The trail continues uphill through a rocky stretch and eventually comes alongside the base of a small bluff.

At 15.8 there are nice boulders scattered along the trail and a larger bluff rising just above the trail on the right. The trail is level for a little while but soon it rises up to the base of the bluff, which is much shorter now, and switchbacks to the RIGHT. It goes up through the bluff and switchbacks to the LEFT on top. Then a nice beautiful, mostly level hike along the top of the bluff.

Soon, the bluff below begins to break down a bit and even disappears and the trail eases uphill a little bit, then back level as the bluff appears again below. At 15.95 we cross a little creek and there's a 23' unnamed waterfall below. Then a little ways beyond, we come to a little creek at the top of Saw-Whet Owl Falls at 16.0, which is a really nice waterfall and is 43' tall. Definitely an SSS, but CAREFUL if trying to get a view along the edge! (It is possible to reach the bottom of the falls by backtracking on the trail to a spot where you can get down through the bluffline and scramble back to the base of the falls.)

Never heard of a Saw-Whet Owl? Me neither. Jim Liles reported these owls in the area while building the trail in the fall and it seemed like a fitting name for the waterfall. As I was working on this part of the guidebook I was also trying to learn how to oil paint. Quite by accident one of the first learn-how-to-paint books I got had a painting lesson of guess what—a Saw-Whet Owl! Small owl, interesting call. Take a break or two through this area and listen...

From the top of the falls, step across the creek and the trail TURNS RIGHT and follows the little creek uphill, then RIGHT across the creek, then heads uphill across another little creek that feeds the waterfall. The trail continues to climb and then swings back to the LEFT and goes up through a rocky area above the little drainages, (usually dry). The trail continues easing uphill, winding around through exposed limestone boulders and chert (limestone gravel).

At 16.3 the trail is still climbing and rounds a bend. During leaf-off there are SSS views through here looking down at the River, upstream and downstream (I saw a flock of giant trumpeter swans on the River from here once). By 16.6. the trail is almost level for a bit and the views keep getting better! This is a nice pleasant walk along a beautiful trail.

Soon the trail swings to the right, leaves the view and the hillside, and drops down into a small ravine. The grade gets a little steeper as the trail winds around on up the hill past 17.0.

The trail turns away from the River for the last time and swings around to the right. You can see a road straight ahead through the trees—that's the road past the trailhead that goes down and dead ends at the South Maumee campground. We head up the hill at a pretty good clip towards the trailhead and come out to South Maumee Road at 17.3.

To reach the trail from Hwy. 27 at Morning Star (between Marshall and Harriet), turn onto CR#52/South Maumee Road (signed, road paved for the first few miles) and go 5.0 miles and park (this is about 1/2 mile past the Buffalo River boundary sign). GPS 36.02344, -92.61695

The trailhead is currently just a wide spot in the road with limited parking, but there will be a real trailhead there soon, we hope.

The trail description continues on past across the road and heads to the Dillards Ferry Trailhead on Hwy. 14 as Section Eleven on the next page. ENJOY!

SECTION ELEVEN — 11.3 miles
S. Maumee Rd. to Hwy. 14/Dillards Ferry (11.3 miles)

Trail Point	Mile Point	Mileage West–East	Mileage East–West
South Maumee Road TH	**196.3**	**0.0**	**11.3**
Maumee Falls East	197.2	.9	10.4
Spring Creek	199.6	3.3	8.0
CR#99 (Spring Creek Rd)	201.6	5.3	6.0
Kimball Creek	205.0	8.7	2.6
Hwy. 14/Dillards Ferry TH	207.6	11.3	0.0

This is one of the most spectacular sections of the OHT/BRT, with several waterfalls and lots of great views down to the River from on top of tall bluffs. Sorry, NO DOGS.

To reach the trail from Hwy. 27 at Morning Star (between Marshall and Harriet), turn onto CR#52/South Maumee Road (should be a big sign on the hwy.) and go 5.0 miles and park (this is about .5 miles past the Buffalo River boundary sign). Limited parking. The trail begins on the RIGHT. CR#52 dead-ends at the Maumee South primitive campground and River access.

The trail heads out on the level across a steep hillside. You can look nearly straight down towards the River, and the leaf-off views are great. At .3 the trail veers away from the River and dips down and back to the right a bit, then curves back to the left, down through a small bluffline. The trail levels out and follows the top of a bluffline (past two wet-weather waterfalls that pour over the bluff below), over to Maumee Falls West, an SSS at .75 (53' tall). At .9 you come to Maumee Falls East (67' tall), another wonderful SSS. You are hiking on top of all these waterfalls, but still have good views as you approach.

From Maumee Falls the trail crosses the creek, turns to the right, heads uphill, and follows the creek upstream. During high water there is at least one waterfall pouring over a smaller bluffline above to the right. The trail veers to the left and comes to the base of that bluffline, an SSS with perhaps another waterfall during high water, and lots of moss-covered boulders too.

The trail continues uphill, then eventually levels off a bit. It swings around a very steep hillside for the next half mile (mostly on the level), and there are some good leaf-off views. At 1.7 you cross the end of a small pond, then curve away to the left, back towards the River. The trail winds around a bit and eventually lands on top of another bluffline, and comes to a nice wet-weath-

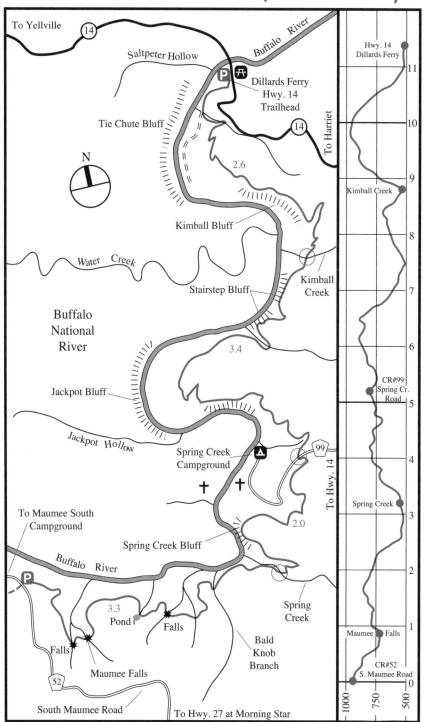

To Yellville

(14)

Buffalo River

Saltpeter Hollow

P 🅿 🏕

Dillards Ferry
Hwy. 14
Trailhead

Tie Chute Bluff

(14)

To Harriet

N

2.6

Kimball Bluff

Water Creek

Stairstep Bluff

Kimball Creek

Kimball
Creek

Buffalo
National
River

Jackpot Bluff

3.4

Jackpot Hollow

CR#99
Spring Cr.
Road

Spring Creek
Campground

▲

(99)

To Hwy. 14

Spring Creek

To Maumee South
Campground

Spring Creek Bluff

2.0

Buffalo River

P 🅿

3.3
Pond

Falls

Spring
Creek

Falls

Bald
Knob
Branch

Maumee Falls

(52)

South Maumee Road

To Hwy. 27 at Morning Star

CR#52
S. Maumee Road

Maumee Falls

Hwy. 14
Dillards Ferry

Kimball Creek

1000   750   500

11
10
9
8
7
6
5
4
3
2
1
0

er waterfall (45' tall) right at the 2.0 mile point, an SSS for sure!

The trail continues along the top of the bluffline, joins an old roadbed and runs mostly level for a while, then eases downhill. At 2.3 the trail/road TURNS LEFT and heads down through the broken bluff at a pretty good clip. It swings to the right, then left, levels some, then back downhill again. The forest turns to bamboo, and at 2.7 crosses Bald Knob Branch. From there the trail/road eases uphill just a little bit, then swings back to the left and levels off. Lots of bamboo in some areas, and the old roadbed disappears and it is back to normal trail again. At 3.1 the trail passes through an old homestead area, then eases downhill a bit (the Buffalo River is just off to the left).

At 3.2 the trail comes alongside Spring Creek and turns right and follows the creek upstream. A beautiful SSS area, lush, with flowing water, a small bluff, and just delightful! The trail crosses the creek at 3.3 (probably a wet crossing), follows the creek for just a little bit and then TURNS LEFT, up and away from the creek. It switchbacks to the right, still heading uphill, then passes under a wet-weather waterfall just above the trail on the left at 3.5. Then the trail switchbacks UP to the left and then continues on the level along the top of the bluffline, passing through several limestone-cedar glades.

There are some nice views along this stretch of trail where each glade opens up the trees a bit, even better during leaf-off. The trail eventually turns away from the top of the bluff and heads uphill. At 4.1 the trail comes out to a spectacular SSS view from on top of Spring Creek Bluff. You've got a terrific open view down to the River, looking directly to the west for a sunset.

The trail curves around to the right and away from the River, mostly on the level, and goes across lush hillsides that are covered with ferns in the summertime. There is a neat sinkhole right next to the trail at 4.7. Just past this is a good example of an "N" tree. The trail eases uphill a bit, then back down, to mile 5.0, where you can begin to see Spring Creek Road below through the trees. The trail comes out to and crosses CR#99/Spring Creek Road at 5.3 (it is 1.7 miles out to Hwy. 14).

From the road the trail heads on down the hill a little bit, crosses a small stream, then runs downhill alongside the stream to a neat little waterfall at 5.5. The trail levels out a bit, then eases uphill through a nice glade that was full of wildflowers, butterflies, and cactus when I was there. More winding around brings you to a steep hillside above the River, with some great SSS views beginning at 5.8. Lots of old weathered, twisted cedars. The trail remains mostly level to mile 6.0, where it curves away from the River, but soon returns again for more great views looking directly down on top of the water. Oh, if only to be a bird!

The trail does a bit of up and downing until 6.7 where it TURNS LEFT onto an old road trace and heads down through a bluffline at a pretty good clip, switchbacks to the right, then not quite as steep, still on the old road. The road splits, but just stay straight and on the level (easy to see). By 7.3 the trail has worked itself down to the bottom and runs near the Buffalo River.

At 7.5 the old road turns right and follows a small creek upstream and away from the Buffalo River, then the road kind of disappears and you are back on plain trail again—a neat little area when the water is high, crossing the creek at 7.75. The trail heads to the left and uphill, soon coming out above the Buffalo and leveling out a bit after a pretty good climb, past mile 8.0. The trail veers away from the River, crosses a small stream, climbs up a bit and returns to leaf-off views above the River, going across a steep hillside. At 8.3 you come to a wonderful SSS view from the top of Stairstep Bluff.

The trail swings away from the River and drops on down to and across Kimball Creek at 8.7. This begins the toughest part of this section as the trail switchbacks up and *up* and UP steeply through limestone rock gardens—lots of natural and man-made steps, but the terrain is all UPHILL! The steepness eases up a bit and you are back to normal trail, although still going up. There is a really nice SSS at 9.2 when the trail comes to the base of a bluff.

From the base of the bluff the trail goes on a little bit, then climbs up and switchbacks to the LEFT and then runs level on top of the bluff (heading back towards the River), where there are many great leaf-off views up and down the drainage. And then at 9.4 you come to a beautiful SSS view from on top of Kimball Bluff (the tallest bluff in the area).

The trail remains mostly level with more great views for a little while, then begins to head downhill and away from the River. At 10.3 there is a nice rock garden and then the trail switchbacks down a couple of times before crossing a small creek, and then it crosses the same creek again just a little ways downstream. The trail bottoms out and goes through a bamboo stand and comes out of the woods and hits a road at 10.9—TURN RIGHT and follow this road (uphill at first) through some old fields, and all the way back to the giant parking area that is right next to (and almost underneath) the big Hwy. 14 bridge at 11.3.

This is the current end of continuous trail—it's 207.6 miles back the other direction to Lake Ft. Smith State Park. At some point this trail will continue downstream through the Lower Buffalo Wilderness and connect with the Sylamore Section of the OHT (see next page) and on to the Missouri border!

SYLAMORE SECTION OF OHT—31.6 miles

MILEAGE LOG

Spring Creek Road/Trailhead	0.0
Cross Spring Creek	7.9
Moccasin Spring Trailhead/Hwy. 341 (1st cross)	9.0
Barkshed Road	12.4
Cripple Turkey Trailhead (Jct. N. Sylamore Trail)	**13.9**
Cole Fork	14.3
Brush Creek Trailhead/Hwy. 341 (2nd cross)	18.1
Hwy. 341—3rd crossing	22.4
Hwy. 341—4th crossing	29.6
Matney Knob Trailhead, Hwy. 341	31.6

There are four trailheads along this route (plus one for the North Sylamore Trail along Cripple Turkey Road). To get to the **Spring Creek Trailhead** take Hwy. 14 east from the community of Big Flat about 4 miles and TURN LEFT/NORTH onto Hwy. 341/Push Mtn. Road (paved); go 2.3 miles and TURN LEFT onto Rand Road/FR#1118 (gravel); go 6.5 miles and TURN LEFT onto Spring Creek Road (gravel); and the trailhead will be on the RIGHT after a half mile. (Or take Spring Creek Rd. north from Big Flat for 6 miles—impassible much of the year at the ford of Spring Cr.) To get to the **Moccasin Spring Trailhead** from the Hwy. 14/341 intersection go north on Hwy. 341 for 1.6 miles and TURN RIGHT. To get to the **Brush Creek Trailhead** from the Hwy. 14/341 intersection go north on Hwy. 341 for 10.3 miles and TURN RIGHT. The **Matney Knob Trailhead** is located right on Hwy. 341 less than a mile west of the big bridge across the White River.

We'll begin this hike from the Spring Creek Trailhead. There will be mileposts each mile, and the trail is marked with 2" x 6" white metal blazes. The trail goes *across* the road from the parking area, through a dense stand of cedar trees (you will see many of these ahead!), then gradually works its way up and over a small ridge and up to the base of Dead Dog Bluff, an SSS at 1.3. It follows along the base of the bluff a little while, then leaves the bluffline and crosses the first of many creeks.

The trail remains up on the hillside between Spring Creek and the bluffline, working its way up into and out of many small drainages, crossing little creeks along the way. There are some great SSS views at 2.8 and 4.7, and more of the same bluffline at 4.1 and 5.9. If the water is high and the creeks are running well you will see a number of waterfalls pouring off of the bluffs, and one especially nice one near the trail at 4.5. Throughout most of this area the trail runs mostly level, with some up and downing but nothing too bad.

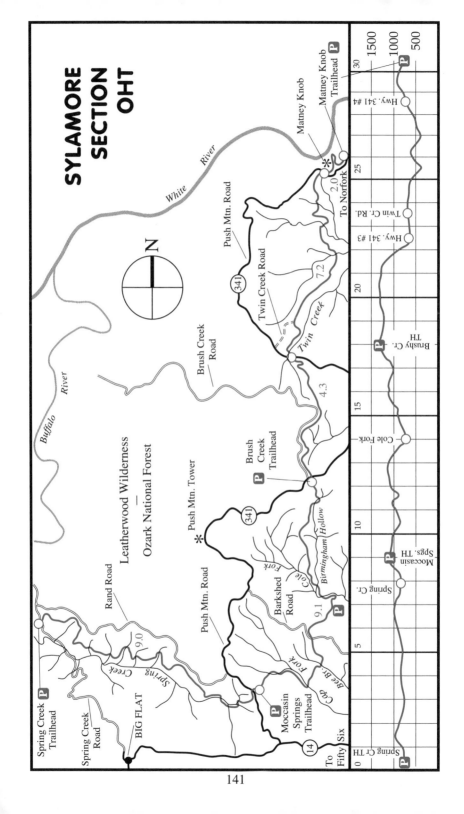

SYLAMORE SECTION OHT

White River

Buffalo River

N

Leatherwood Wilderness
—
Ozark National Forest

Push Mtn. Tower

Rand Road

Spring Creek Trailhead

Spring Creek Road

BIG FLAT

9.0

Spring Creek

Push Mtn. Road

Push Mtn. Road

Brush Creek Road

341

Twin Creek Road

Twin Creek

7.2

4.3

341

Brush Creek Trailhead

Cole Fork

Birmingham Hollow

Barkshed Road

9.1

Bee Br. Fork

Cole Fork

Moccasin Springs Trailhead

14

To Fifty Six

Matney Knob

Matney Knob Trailhead

2.0

To Norfork

1500

1000

500

30

25

20

15

10

5

0

Hwy. 341 #4

Twin Cr. Rd.

Hwy. 341 #3

Brushy Cr. TH

Cole Fork

Moccasin Spgs. TH

Spring Cr.

Spring Cr. TH

141

At 7.2 the trail enters an old clearcut area where it follows an old road through the clearcut, then exits on plain trail straight out into the woods. Soon after the clearcut the trail comes down and runs alongside Spring Creek itself, finally crossing it at 7.9. From that point the trail follows the creek upstream, then crosses it again where the creek forks. Eventually the trail begins to climb up and out of the drainage (via six quick switchbacks), coming alongside Hwy. 341, and crossing it at 9.0.

The trail continues across the road on a jeep road and goes to the right and past Moccasin Spring Trailhead. Stay on the road for another 100 yards past the trailhead and then TURN LEFT off of the road and onto plain trail. From there the trail works its way down into the bottom of a drainage, where it crosses a small stream several times. In between the 3rd and 4th crossings a bluffline on the right comes down to the creek at a place known as Moccasin Springs at 9.9—a neat SSS.

At 10.7 the trail enters a small wildlife food plot, then leaves the food plot at the far end to the LEFT and crosses Cap Creek. It climbs the hill on a four-wheeler trail, crosses a jeep road, then drops down into and across Bee Branch at 11.5. After another climb UP the hillside, the trail intersects a jeep road at 11.9—TURN LEFT and follow this road along the top of the ridge, through two food plots, to Barkshed Road at 12.4. It is plain trail again through the woods until you reach Cripple Turkey Road at 12.9—TURN RIGHT and follow this road for the next 1.1 miles (past a trailhead for the North Sylamore Creek Trail—GPS 36.05655, -92.31844). When you get to the bottom of the hill TURN LEFT onto a four-wheel trail at MILEPOST 14.0. Follow this trail upstream until you TURN RIGHT and cross Cole Fork at 14.3.

From Cole Fork it's normal trail again, as it works its way up onto a ridge between Birmingham Hollow and Cole Fork—SSS rock formations at 14.8 (there are calcite crystal cave formations on the sides of the rocks!), and an SSS view at 15.0. At 15.2 you intersect with Birmingham Road. You will be on this road as it roller-coasters along the top of the ridge for 1.2 miles. Just past the second food plot at 16.4, TURN RIGHT and leave the road and head into the woods on plain trail. From here the trail drops on down the hill and crosses Birmingham Hollow a couple of times (a great SSS waterfall is up on the right at 17.4 just before the second crossing). Then the trail climbs up the hillside and comes out to Hwy. 341 again at the Brush Creek Trailhead at 18.1.

The trail continues across the road, and runs just below Advance Road mostly on the level, and past a couple of nice waterfalls during the wet season (an SSS at 19.2). It eventually veers away from the road, then runs along the top of a ridge, then leaves the ridgetop and drops down to a terrific SSS view at 21.4. Just beyond the trail makes eight switchbacks DOWN the hill, leveling out and crossing Hwy. 341 at 22.2. It soon crosses Twin Creek and follows it downstream a little ways, then swings to the left and intersects with Twin Creek Road at 23.5—TURN RIGHT and follow this road for 2.0 miles. Mostly level country.

The road/trail passes several wildlife food plots, then begins to head downhill (the road gets much worse here). Just as the road levels out some, and before it comes to a private property line, the trail heads out into the woods at 25.5 to the LEFT and continues on as plain trail.

The trail heads down to and across a creek, then climbs back up again and runs along the side of a hill, then drops down to and across Rough Hollow, then back up again, then down to and across one last creek, before making a final climb back out. The trail eases uphill gradually before coming out to the fourth crossing of Hwy. 341 at 28.8.

After you cross the road the trail heads into the woods to the right and switchbacks uphill just a little bit. There is a great SSS view at 29.9, then you come to mile #30. Soon after the viewpoint you come to a road and TURN LEFT onto the road, but just for a little bit. After only 100 yards leave the road TO THE RIGHT and head off into the woods on level trail.

The trail passes under a powerline and across a rocky hillside (all of this area is Matney Knob). At 30.8 you will come out to the edge of the hillside and get a nice view of the White River Valley, and the river itself far below. It is very rocky in this area, and there is not much trail tread, so watch carefully for a switchback where the trail turns back away from the view and into the woods, almost doubling back onto itself. It levels out and passes mile #31.

The trail hits an old road just beyond, and TURNS LEFT and heads downhill on the old road, then levels out. You are now walking next to Hwy. 341. At 31.4 the trail LEAVES THE ROAD TO THE RIGHT, and continues on the level through the woods and comes to the end of the trail at the Matney Knob Trailhead at 31.6. This is also Hwy. 341. If you turn left on the highway here it is only about a half mile to the crossing of the White River.

The OHT route will follow this highway and other roads all the way to the Lake Norfork Dam, where it will join with existing hiking trail for the rest of the trip up to the Missouri border.

SHORES LAKE TO WHITE ROCK LOOP — 13.4 miles total

Shores Lake and White Rock are two of the most popular recreation areas in the Ozark National Forest, located northeast of Ft. Smith. This loop trail runs from Shores Lake, past several nice waterfalls, up to the spectacular White Rock Mountain, then returns to the lake down through the Salt Fork drainage. This is the perfect weekend hike, especially if you are lucky enough to get a cabin at White Rock. Or you can dayhike either side of the loop, if you run a shuttle. The trail gains over 1700 feet in elevation during several good climbs. Bidville quad.

To get to the trailhead, take exit #24 off of I–40 (Mulberry exit), go north on Hwy. 215 past Fern, go 3 miles and turn left at the sign onto FR# 1505 (paved, County Road 75), go to almost the end of the pavement and turn right into the campground and follow the signs to the trailhead. The trail is blazed blue.

 The trail begins at the signboard and heads out through the rocky forest, then splits — TURN LEFT on the *West Side Loop* (we'll return on the *East Side Loop* from the right). It crosses FR# 1505, and continues into the woods along a rocky trail. It soon drops down a bench or two, crossing a couple of old log roads. (A tornado damaged much of this loop in 1996.)

It then makes its way into and across a boulder-strewn Bliss Spring Hollow. Cross the creek just upstream, then bear left as the trail heads uphill. It passes MILE MARKER #1. These mile markers show mileage back to Shores Lake. Up to this point, the trail was in the Hurricane Creek drainage. From #1 it turns more to the north and heads up into, and will run alongside White Rock Creek. Along the way, the trail drops down into the bottom and crosses two wooden bridges. Just after these, the trail intersects with a four-wheeler road and TURNS RIGHT on it.

While on the road, you come right next to the creek. Before too long the trail leaves the road TO THE RIGHT. The trail heads uphill for a short distance, then levels off and continues to follow the creek upstream, looking right down onto it.

It comes back down to the creek, and intersects the road again. TURN RIGHT and continue on the road. There is a large boulder or two here. Nice spot. Just before the road crosses the creek, TURN RIGHT off of the road and head into the woods again. It takes off up a rather steep grade, but levels off before too long, and then looks down on the creek again.

The trail crosses a small creek, then goes up another short,

Shores Lake/White Rock Loop–13.4 mi.

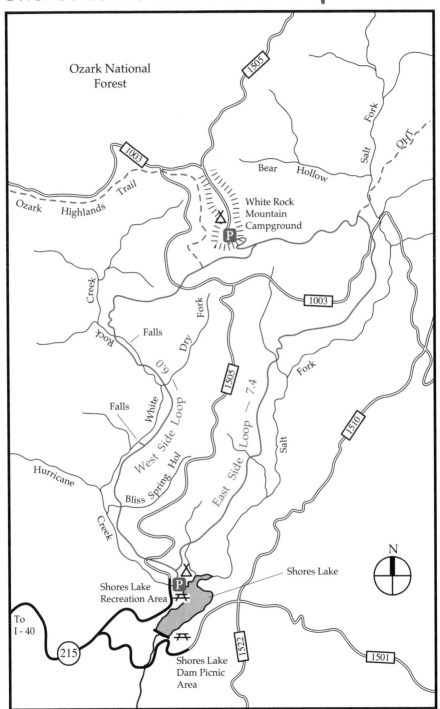

Ozark National Forest

1505

Bear Hollow

Salt Fork

OHT

1003

Ozark Highlands Trail

White Rock Mountain Campground

P

1003

Rock Creek

Falls

Dry Fork

6.0

1505

East Side Loop – 7.4

Salt Fork

1510

Falls

White

West Side Loop

Bliss Spring Hol

Hurricane

Creek

N

Shores Lake

Shores Lake Recreation Area

P

To I - 40

215

1522

1501

Shores Lake Dam Picnic Area

steep grade. Before too long you come to a trail intersection. The sign says that there is a waterfall in both directions. If you turn left and go downhill (not blazed), you'll climb down to White Rock Creek and a real nice waterfall that spans the creek, about a class B falls. The main trail GOES STRAIGHT at the intersection.

It continues across a bench, and works its way down to and across Dry Creek. Just beyond, the trail intersects with a four-wheeler road again. TURN RIGHT here and follow the road. A hundred yards or so down the road the trail TURNS LEFT and cuts across a corner in the road, rejoining the road. A little ways further the trail leaves the road for good TO THE LEFT.

It comes alongside White Rock Creek again, close to a couple of giant boulders, and crosses the creek at 2.75. The trail crosses just upstream and then follows the creek a couple of hundred feet and then comes to the second falls on this section at 2.8. This class B falls is one of my SSS's. The pool here is generally swimmable all year, and makes for a great rest stop!

The trail goes up and around the falls to the left, and then continues upstream, past a primitive camp area on the left. It then drops down and crosses White Rock Creek again at 2.9. During high water, you can save these two creek crossings but there is a pretty good climb on the other side of the falls. Both of these crossings can be crossed dry most of the year, but you may have to look around a while for a suitable crossing.

Once across the creek, the trail turns upstream and continues level. Then it turns to the right a couple of times, passes MILE MARKER #3, and heads up a steep grade. At about the point where the trail levels off, you can bushwhack down below the trail, on around the hill and into a nice little side canyon. Here you will find "Hidden Falls" (class D), a wonderful SSS.

Stay on the trail, and you will also come around the hill into a little ravine, and cross a small stream just below a couple of class B waterfalls. *Caution* — don't go downstream to the head of Hidden Falls — it is real slick and a long fall! Across the stream the trail works its way up another small rocky drainage. It eventually crosses it, and continues to work its way uphill.

The trail levels off a little bit, then runs along the edge of a clearcut area that is visible off to the right. It works its way around the clearcut area, gradually heading uphill.

Eventually, the trail heads uphill at a more serious pace. Back behind you there are some nice views. But the trail continues *up*.

It veers away from the cut area for a short, level rest, then picks up the steep climb again. This is one of the worst climbs on the trail. It continues uphill for what seems like an eternity.

At last, the trail makes a sharp turn to the right, and levels off a bit. It is still heading uphill, but not near as steep. You can look ahead a long ways here and see that the trail continues at about the same grade. And then you pass MILE MARKER #4. Beyond #4 the grade gets a little steeper and then goes up and over a small hill, and you drop down into a low area.

Then it's up another small rise, where the trail intersects a jeep road. TURN LEFT on this road for about 50 feet, then TURN RIGHT off of the road back onto trail again. It runs down and across another low area. All of this area around here is easily accessible and used a lot by hunters. Lots of camp spots. The trail crosses another jeep road, and then crosses FR# 1003 at 4.5.

From here the trail runs on an old roadbed, heading uphill. It levels off a bit, then continues up. It swings around to the left of a small ridge, then makes it's way on top of the ridge and levels off. The trail intersects with the main trail at 4.8 (white blazes). If you turn left here it will take you back to Lake Ft. Smith State Park. TURN RIGHT and continue on the old road to White Rock.

The old road works its way around a small hill, then begins to descend. There is a great view of the bluff above from here. The roadbed disappears as the trail drops down to and across a small creek, then works its way up the other side. It climbs up and around a small hill, and passes OHT mile 17.0 — this is of course the mileage back to Lake Ft. Smith State Park.

From here the trail runs on a fairly level grade, with some up–and–downing. Then it works its way up to another trail intersection at 5.65. The right-hand fork is the main trail and continues to the east down into the Salt Fork drainage. TURN LEFT and head up the hill towards White Rock (blue blazes again). The trail passes a trail register (use it) and then works its way up through the bluffline. Once on top, TURN LEFT and follow the trail on the ridgetop out to a dead–end road and a row of cabins. The trailhead lot is just ahead on the right at 6.0. The whole place is an SSS. Rent a cabin or the lodge and really enjoy your stay. They are open all year. Call 479–369–4128.

Now lets head back down the trail for a quick trip to Shores Lake (7.4 miles). Head down the same spur trail that you came up on, and TURN LEFT at the OHT intersection (white blazes again) — we'll keep the mileage total running to include this spur — so this will be 6.4. The trail heads steeply down the hill, past some nice big trees, winding down off of the hillside. It runs on a jeep road part of the way. At 8.0 (near OHT mile 19.0), TURN RIGHT off of the OHT and head off level — this is the *East Side Loop*. This runs on over to a spur trail at 8.7 (it goes up a rocky hillside to the right to an SSS waterfall) — continue STRAIGHT here and cross FR# 1003 just beyond.

This next section of trail is especially nice during leaf–off, 'cause the views are wonderful. It runs along mostly level, but dropping just a little. It drops on down to and across a creek at 10.5, then heads up to another SSS waterfall, and then joins a jeep road — TURN LEFT and run along the road a half mile to 11.2, then TURN LEFT off of the road. The trail runs along a steep hillside — lots of SSS views, then runs level for a while. It heads up the hill past a wonderful SSS area of boulders and huge trees, then drops on down the hillside and back to the intersection with the West Loop at 13.3. TURN LEFT here and return to the trailhead, for a total loop of 13.4 miles.

WHITE ROCK RIM LOOP — 2.1 miles total

This is easily one of the most scenic hikes in Arkansas — *all* of it a definite SSS!!! The trail follows along the top of the bluffline up on White Rock Mountain. Along the trail you will find a great spot to watch the sunrise, and what I consider the best sunset in the entire state. The views are spectacular all year.

This is a great getaway spot too — there are three cabins available for rent, as well as a "lodge" that sleeps up to 28, and a campground. Although this is a real easy trail to hike, nearly level all the way, you should not take small children with you – the risk of a fatal fall is just too great. To optimize the views, the trail runs close to the edge of the tall bluff most of the way. It's not a good idea to hike after dark (it is closed after sunset), or while intoxicated — there have been a number of deaths related to these factors in the past few years. Bidville quad.

There are many ways to get to White Rock — see page 45 for the description of the route that has the least amount of dirt road. Once you get into the recreation area, go past the campground to where the road forks — turn left and go past the Lodge and cabins and park at the OHT trailhead on the left (red one on map). This is where the Rim Loop Trail description begins.

White Rock Rim Loop — 2.1 miles

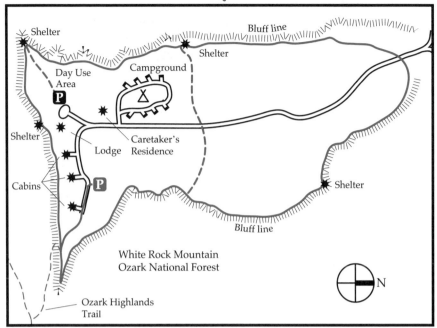

Shelter

Bluff line

Shelter

Day Use Area

Campground

P

Shelter

Caretaker's Residence

Lodge

Cabins

P

Shelter

Bluff line

White Rock Mountain
Ozark National Forest

N

Ozark Highlands
Trail

(text begins on previous page) ***Head down this same road*** on foot, past the last cabin — the trail takes off at the end of the road. As it runs on out towards the end of the point, a trail comes in from the right — this is where we'll finish this loop — go STRAIGHT AHEAD to the second intersection. The OHT takes off to the right here, but we want to once again continue STRAIGHT AHEAD. The trail from this point on is not marked or blazed, but it is easy to follow. Soon beyond, the trail comes to the end of the point and swings sharply back to the left — this point is a good spot to watch the sunrise during leaf–off.

As the trail heads on around on top of the bluff, you get some great views down onto the bluff itself — lots of lichen and moss and even a few ferns growing on the rock. By the way, this is a sandstone bluff. The drainage out in front of you is the Salt Fork Creek valley. The trail continues to hug the bluff, going past several large hardwood trees. At .4 the trail passes by a wonderful rock well cover. There are a number of open views through here. In fact, you can look out across Salt Fork to the first mountain beyond, which is Potato Knob Mountain, and see six or seven ridges past that. Needless to say, all of this is an SSS!

Please remember to watch your step as you soak up everything.

At .8 there is a lesser cutoff trail that heads up the hill to the left — this is a short trail that goes up to the entrance road near the campground, and on over to the Rim Trail on the other side. At .9 the trail comes to one of the four rock pavilions along the trail — another fine example of CCC work. This is another great spot to watch the sunrise. Just beyond this shelter, you'll see a lot of rocks both above and below the trail that are covered with a thick carpet of moss — a special SSS area.

The trail swings away from the bluff to the left some at 1.0, then comes out onto the forest road that leads up to White Rock at 1.1. TURN LEFT and head up this road for just a hundred feet or so, then turn off of the road TO THE RIGHT, back on trail again. There was no sign here, so be alert for the trail. It continues along pretty level, passes under a power line, and then joins the top of the bluff on this west side at 1.2. You'll have a great view to the west from this point on for a while — a super SSS all the way! The trail eventually heads up a flight of steps and actually goes right through the second pavilion at 1.3. The cutoff trail that we passed on the other side joins us here — it goes up to the entrance road and down to the Rim Trail on the other side. Just past this spot there are a couple of other trails to the left that go up to the campground.

One of the best views is along here looking to the south at the rest of the bluffline out in front of you — and the third pavilion that is perched out on it in the distance. Everywhere is a great sunset view too. And a spectacular spot to view the colors in late October. The trail makes its way on over to that third pavilion at 1.7 — the wide trail there that heads up the hill to the left goes into the picnic area (and toilets) and day use parking. This is perhaps the most scenic, and popular spot on the mountain. No need to explain why. Our trail wraps around the point, swinging back to the left, and heads to the fourth and final pavilion at 1.8. This last stretch of trail runs just below the lodge and cabins, and there is at least one trail that goes up to each one of them.

As the trail makes its way to the east below the cabins, there are still some nice views to the south. After passing the last cabin, the trail swings left and intersects with the beginning of our loop at 2.0 — TURN LEFT and head back up to the trailhead. The complete loop is 2.1 miles total.

Redding/Spy Rock Loop — 8.8 miles

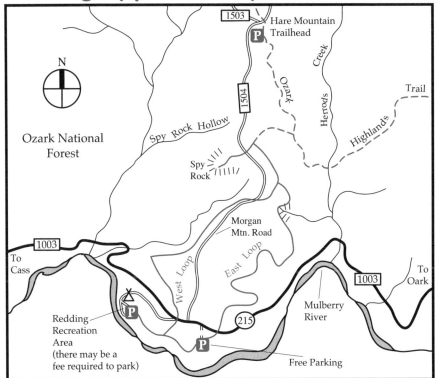

REDDING/SPY ROCK LOOP — 8.8 miles total

This is one of four loop trails that connect with the OHT. It passes several nice waterfalls, and has a spur that goes out to a neat view spot called Spy Rock. Many folks use this trail to access the OHT. It's also a good dayhike, eating lunch at Spy Rock. Redding Campground is a popular area with floaters who use the Mulberry River. There are 27 campsites, flush toilets and showers (in season), and water. There may be a fee to park at the trailhead—but a free one is located nearby (see map).

To get to Redding, go just north of the community of Cass on Hwy. 23 (the Pig Trail), turn east onto paved FR# 1003/Hwy. 215, go about 3 miles and turn right on the Redding Campground access road (or go past this turnoff and turn right onto Huggins Road to get to the free parking area). The parking area ($) is located in the campground next to the river. Cass quad.

The trail begins in the campground at the parking area that is shared with the river folks. It winds through the campground, past the bathhouse, and across the road into the woods. It is marked with blue blazes. The trail takes off TO

THE RIGHT down a wide corridor that is actually the sewer line.
It leaves this wide corridor TO THE RIGHT and continues through
a stand of pine trees. These were planted in 1962. If you look
around a bit you can see the rows that the trees were planted in. In
fact the trail goes right down some of these rows.

It winds around in the bottom, crosses an old roadbed, then
comes to an intersection at .6. The left fork becomes the *West Side
Loop*. The trail that goes straight ahead is the *East Side Loop*. We
will go up the West Side Loop, on out to Spy Rock, and come
back down the East Side Loop, so TURN LEFT here.

The West Loop runs alongside the stand of pines and comes
out to and crosses FR# 1003 (paved) at the campground entrance
at .8. It begins to climb up the hill into the woods. It winds
around, past MILEPOST #1, then swings up and across a ridge.
It turns right and continues climbing gradually, past MILEPOST
#2. It swings back to the left, and runs just below FR# 1505.

In this area there is a pine tree marked with two blue blazes
in the shape of a cross. Just down the hill from this spot is a large
dug/blasted–out hole with an old cable around it. *Caution:* If
you have a dog or kids with you make sure that they stay well
away from the edge — a fall could be fatal. I won't go into the
complete story about this hole, but here is the short version.
It was dug (like many others in the area) by locals that were
looking for a pot of gold that the Spanish buried somewhere
around when the area was first explored. "Spy Rock" got its
name from this same era — a lookout was stationed there while
the others buried the gold!

As the trail makes its way around the hill to the right you can
look out to the north and see a rock outcrop at the end of a small
ridge—this is Spy Rock. There is a spur trail on this route that
runs out the top of that ridge to the nice view there. We continue
level around the hill, past MILEPOST #3, then across FR# 1505 at
3.2. The trail climbs up and over a hill, crosses an old road, and
intersects with the East Side Loop at 3.6 (it's 3.6 miles back to the
campground via the East Side Loop — 7.2 miles total loop).
We're going to TURN LEFT here and head towards Spy Rock
and the main OHT. The trail towards Spy Rock heads off down
into the woods. It eventually eases up the hill just a little, then
comes to a trail intersection at 4.0. TURN LEFT to go to Spy Rock.
(If you turned right, you would head on over, down the hill just
a little, and intersect with the main OHT after a little more than
a half mile — page 63.) The trail crosses FR# 1504, then runs on

out the top of the ridge to Spy Rock at 4.4, and a terrific SSS view down into the Mulberry River Valley.

Now lets hike back to the West–East Loop intersection — I'm keeping a running mileage total that includes the trip out to Spy Rock and back, so back to this intersection would be 5.2 total so far for the hike. We'll take the East Side Loop back. The East Side Loop makes its way on around the hill, down past an SSS view during leaf–off and passing a nice SSS waterfall at 5.7. There is a lot of neat stuff growing at the base of this falls — if you can only figure out how to get down and have a look at it! (The trail eventually passes MILEPOST #3, which is the mileage to Redding). It drops down and skirts around a regeneration area — be alert to where the trail is going. Good SSS leaf-off views.

It begins to drop down the hill, past another SSS waterfall at 6.7, (MILEPOST #2 is just beyond), and continues to work its way down the hill. It eventually crosses FR# 1003 at 7.7. Just beyond, TURN LEFT onto a jeep road for a hundred feet, then TURN RIGHT, through the free parking area and down into the woods. (Park here and bypass the campground and the parking fee there.) It winds up in the bottoms close to the Mulberry River, and eventually makes its way back to the intersection with the West Side Loop at 8.2. GO STRAIGHT AHEAD here, and follow the trail back to Redding. The total loop is 8.8 miles.

GPS WAYPOINT COORDINATES

GPS coordinates for some of the most important locations along the OHT. Set your GPS to digital/decimal degrees, WGS 84.

	Mile Point	Coordinates	
Lake Ft. Smith Trailhead	0.0	35.69578	-94.11925
Frog Bayou (west crossing)	2.9	35.71478	-94.11304
Jacks Cr. Four-Wheeler Road	5.0	35.70517	-94.09190
Dockerys Gap TH/FR# 1007	9.3	35.70706	-94.03782
Hurricane Creek	10.0	35.70319	-94.03219
FR# 1703	13.2	35.69415	-93.99575
Woods Gap /FR# 1003/1505	15.1	35.69776	-93.96867
White Rock Mtn. Trailhead	spur	35.68953	-93.95447
Shores Lake Trailhead	spur	35.64456	-93.96035
Salt Fork Creek	19.2	35.69873	-93.93279
Potato Knob Mtn./FR# 1510	21.3	35.70164	-93.91495
Spirits Creek	23.6	35.68521	-93.90632
Ragtown Road/FR# 1509	24.8	35.68374	-93.89797
Fane Creek	30.3	35.69996	-93.83461
Fane Creek Road/FR# 1520	30.4	35.70055	-93.83432
Cherry Bend TH/Hwy. 23	35.5	35.74337	-93.81152
E. Fly Gap Road /FR# 1503	39.1	35.74411	-93.77711
Hare Mountain	41.3	35.74834	-93.75679
Hare Mtn/Morgan Fields TH	43.1	35.72593	-93.75531
Herrods Creek	46.2	35.69932	-93.74834
Indian Creek	50.0	35.69369	-93.71273
Indian Creek TH/Hwy. 215	spur	35.68368	-93.71049
Lick Branch Trailhead	55.1	35.71000	-93.66157
Little Mulberry Creek Bridge	56.9	35.70085	-93.64103
FR# 1453/CR# 6200	64.7	35.73773	-93.55950
Lynn Hollow Creek	69.1	35.75096	-93.53521
Arbaugh Road TH/FR# 1404	70.0	35.75774	-93.52792
Lewis Prong Creek, west	72.0	35.73854	-93.51342
Moonhull Mountain	77.5	35.74088	-93.46386

	Mile Point	Coordinates	
Boomer Branch	81.0	35.71062	-93.45437
Mulberry River	83.3	35.68832	-93.45009
FR# 1003/CR# 5440	83.4	35.68722	-93.45000
Ozone Trailhead/Hwy. 21	84.7	35.67296	-93.45064
Little Piney River, 1st cross	87.0	35.67852	-93.42677
FR# 1405/CR# 5550	88.3	35.68607	-93.40993
Lick Creek	92.3	35.67450	-93.36553
FR# 1004/CR# 5671 TH	94.3	35.66641	-93.34686
Cedar Creek Pool	96.7	35.68252	-93.33082
FR# 1003/CR# 5680 TH	97.9	35.68956	-93.31696
Gee Creek	100.6	35.68395	-93.28147
Hwy. 123 to Haw Creek CG	102.1	35.67931	-93.25977
Big Piney/Ft. Douglas TH	103.8	35.67790	-93.23812
Highwater Bypass Trail	107.8	35.71403	-93.21188
Hurricane Creek, west cross	109.4	35.71456	-93.22490
Natural Bridge	109.9	35.71897	-93.22392
Greasy Creek	112.0	35.72445	-93.19791
Hurricane Creek, east cross	113.4	35.72264	-93.18289
Chancel Trailhead	spur	35.75404	-93.14151
4-wheel rd/Buck Branch	121.8	35.74131	-93.11802
Fairview Trailhead/ Hwy. 7	123.8	35.73875	-93.09376
FR# 1255/CR # 5000	126.1	35.74822	-93.06945
Richland Creek cross #1	133.2	35.76381	-92.98738
Moore CCC Trailhead	spur	35.77285	-92.98908
Ben Hur/Moore Trailhead	134.5	35.75371	-92.98234
FR# 1203/CR# 5050	135.0	35.74942	-92.97835
Falling Water Creek	138.4	35.75264	-92.93826
Richland Creek CG TH	143.1	35.79649	-92.93826
Stack Rock TH/FR# 1201	150.8	35.86670	-92.92997
Dry Creek	152.9	35.86906	-92.94531
Buffalo River (Woolum)	164.0	35.96991	-92.88720

(continues on next page)

	Mile Point	Coordinates	
Richland Creek cross #3	164.2	35.96821	-92.88941
Point Peter Mountain	165.2	35.96518	-92.88566
Ben Branch	167.5	35.95676	-92.86253
Dave Manes Bluff	168.0	35.95727	-92.85430
Hage Hollow Creek	170.1	35.95752	-92.83900
Whisenant Hollow Bluffs	171.3	35.95278	-92.82754
Tie Slide	173.2	35.95924	-92.80583
Calf Creek	176.3	35.97170	-92.77108
Collier Homestead TH	177.1	35.97526	-92.76543
Tyler Bend VC (via spur)	178.5	35.98619	-92.76331
Grinders Ferry TH/Hwy. 65	179.0	35.98420	-92.74422
Long Bottom Road	180.6	35.98396	-92.73158
Illinois Point	180.9	35.98446	-92.72737
Amphitheater Falls	181.7	35.98368	-92.72624
Bear Creek	184.8	35.98995	-92.70371
Zack Ridge Road Trailhead	185.6	35.99087	-92.69601
Brush Creek	186.7	35.99734	-92.68859
Red Bluff Spur Trail	187.5	36.00662	-92.68138
Red Bluff Road Trailhead	190.1	36.01624	-92.65714
Rocky Creek	192.0	36.01708	-92.64338
Little Rocky Creek	193.3	36.00945	-92.63524
Pileated Point	193.5	36.01135	-92.63634
Hoot-Owl Hollow	194.7	36.01154	-92.62123
Saw-Whet Owl Falls	195.0	36.01502	-92.62017
South Maumee Road TH	196.3	36.02344	-92.61695
Maumee Falls East	197.2	36.01651	-92.61032
Spring Creek	199.6	36.01818	-92.58530
CR#99 (Spring Creek Road)	201.6	36.02864	-92.57985
Kimball Creek	205.0	36.04718	-92.57307
Dillards Ferry TH/Hwy. 14	207.6	36.0652	-92.5783

OHT SYLAMORE SECTION

	Mile Point	Coordinates	
Spring Creek Rd/Trailhead	0.0	36.05300	-92.44502
Cross Spring Creek	7.9	36.02545	-92.36580
Moccasin Spring TH/Hwy. 341 (1st crossing)			
	9.0	36.02982	-92.35290
Barkshed Road	12.4	36.04539	-92.32773
Cripple Turkey TH	13.9	36.05655	-92.31844
Cole Fork	14.3	36.05990	-92.32123
Brush Creek TH/Hwy. 341 (2nd crossing)			
	18.1	36.10047	-92.32682
Hwy. 341—3rd crossing	22.4	36.14158	-92.33568
Hwy. 341—4th crossing	29.6	36.20482	-92.32107
Matney Knob TH Hwy. 341	31.6	36.21422	-92.30818

HIKING CLUBS

The best way to get involved with trails is to join one or more of the following outdoor organizations. They all have regular meetings, and sponsor frequent hikes and other outings, including volunteer work trips — many to the OHT. This is your chance to meet other hikers from your area, and to get out and explore the outdoors.

OZARK HIGHLANDS TRAIL ASSOCIATION
P. O. Box 4065
Fayetteville, AR 72702
www.OzarkHighlandsTrail.com
ohta@OzarkHighlandsTrail.com

Ouachita Mountain Hikers
Hot Springs
www.omhikers.net

Friends of the Ouachita Trail (FoOT)
Hot Springs
www.FriendsOT.org

Ozark Society
Little Rock
www.OzarkSociety.net

Arkansas Sierra Club
Little Rock
www.Arkansas.SierraClub.org

TakAHik
Russellville
www.TakaHik.com

TrailBlazers Hiking Club
Ft. Smith
www.thcfs.com

Arkansas Trails Council
www.ArkansasTrailsCouncil.com

ABOUT THE AUTHOR

Tim Ernst is a native of Fayetteville and lifelong resident of his most favorite state, Arkansas.

He made his first backpacking trip in the spring of 1974 with a Wal Mart backpack and an army surplus mummy bag filled with chicken feathers. There were no hiking trails back then. He bushwhacked alone following creeks, ridges, and a few forest roads for 125 miles from Lake Ft. Smith State Park to near the community of Ben Hur. The route he pioneered then became the framework for the Ozark Highlands Trail.

His latest long journey was just this past February (2021), when he became the first to travel on foot from the source of the mighty Buffalo River high in the Ozarks, to the mouth of the Buffalo at the White River— some 150+ miles downstream. (A two-week trek, about half established trail and half bushwhacking along the river corridor.)

In the meantime Tim has produced twenty coffee table picture books during a 46-year nature photography career, which included a few hikes along the way.

Who would have guessed that he would meet his lovely bride, Pamela, on a hike (and daughter, Amber). They've been married for more than 20 years now and live in the woods near Jasper not far from the OHT, with springer spaniel pups Mia and Wilson.

MAP LEGEND

————	Main Described Trail	▬▬▬▬	Paved Highway
- - - - -	Other Trails	═══════	Dirt / Gravel Road
O—1.3—O	Mileage Between Points	= = = = =	Jeep Road
P	Trailhead Parking	(59)	Federal Highway
⋀	Campground	(88)	State Highway
⊼	Day Use Area	(324)	County Road
†	Cemetery	[132]	Forest Road
		\\\\\||||////||	Bluff

Mileage log for entire trail is on pages 32–34
GPS waypoints are on pages 154–157

Ozark Highlands Trail

www.TimErnst.com